"With 'Ayyam al-Habib (The Life and the Prophet Muhammad (peace upon him) based on authentic Muslim sources, Dr. Ahmed Bangura and Mustafa Al-Hamadani have provided a great service to Muslims and members of other faith communities. The original Arabic work provides a brief but moving description of the major milestones and most significant events defining the career of the last Prophet. It does far more though. The book's extensive annotation explains uncommon Arabic terms, thereby providing very valuable linguistic, etymological and semantic insights. Hence, in addition to its general appeal to Arabic readers, this book will prove extremely useful to students of the Arabic language.

'Indelible Footprints', the lucid English translation makes this important work available to westerners seeking to more fully understand the Prophet Muhammad's (peace upon him) life and legacy at a time both are being distorted, sometimes for nefarious purposes. I highly recommend this timely volume."

– Imam Zaid Shakir,
Scholar and co-founder of Zaytuna College

~

"This beautiful translation of stories and anecdotes about the life and teachings of the Prophet Muhammad, told through the voices of his followers, wives, and even some antagonists, gives us illuminating glimpses into the simple profundity of the religion he espoused. The narratives furthered my understanding of the times and context in which he lived, and also my appreciation for the many pearls of the wisdom scattered throughout his words and deeds. 'And everyone's neighbor is as precious as oneself' is just one of many of such passages. I hope to try to emulate such selflessness in my own life."

– Stephen Roddy, Professor of Modern and Classical Languages,
University of San Francisco

~

"'Indelible Footprints' is the kind of book you pick up, turn to any page and inevitably find timeless inspiration. Each story provides relevant and fascinating glimpses into the exemplary character of the Prophet Muhammad. This is a very captivating book."

– Ashley Hart, former student of Ahmed Bangura;
now living in Singapore

Indelible Footprints

Stories from the life of Prophet Muhammad

Ahmed Sheikh Bangura

Córdoba
Books

ISBN-13: 978-1724980557
ISBN-10: 1724980556

CreateSpace Independent Publishing Platform
United States of America

Contents

Contents

Contents

~

Preface

The book, *"Indelible Footprints: Short stories from the Life of the Prophet Muhammad,"* contains a selection of key episodes from the life of the Prophet Muhammad (peace be upon him). It is an abridged translation of *Ayyam al-Habib* (*Days of the Beloved*), which I co-authored, and which has been published in Arabic. *"Indelible Footprints: Short stories from the Life of the Prophet Muhammad"* also features a sampling of the Prophet's (pbuh) stories and supplications.

For the biographical section, which is the core of the book, I have included eyewitness accounts related both in the books of *Hadith* (Prophetic traditions) and in Islam's early books of history and biography—*Magazi* and *Seera*, respectively.

There are supplementary introductions to the chapters concerning the Prophet's stories and supplications.

There are many modern biographies on the life of the Prophet, but these, as detailed as they might get, do not usually give the reader adequate access to the original reports upon which they are based.

This book is a modest attempt at presenting some of the original texts themselves, so that the reader can have a special connection with the words and styles of the narrators, and perhaps more significantly with what many Muslims believe to be the words and actions of the Prophet Muhammad (pbuh) and those of the people with whom he interacted throughout his life. I have tried to divide the biographical section into segments of the Prophet's (pbuh) life; starting from his early childhood to his death, but the texts themselves do not always follow a strictly chronological order.

I have been very selective in what to include in this volume. This is inevitable given the nearly inexhaustible pool of material available on one of history's most documented lives. Also, I have chosen texts that can stand on their own, and do not require lengthy contextual explanations and commentaries. Furthermore, I consider the episodes included here as representing what is constant in the Prophet's conduct, and not his special responses to extraordinary circumstances.

It has taken nearly fifteen years to gather these stories. The temptation to keep sifting for more material has been great, but I now feel the need to share what I have so far with others.

The Prophet's (pbuh) stories and supplications also provide a unique access to the values the Prophet (pbuh) taught and the issues that he faced in the course of his life.

I am grateful to all the people who have contributed to this work. The responses of my students at the University of San Francisco to the manuscript over the years have been very useful. I thank them for their insights. Sheikh Moukhtar Maghraoui provided a great deal of inspiration for this effort, for which I am grateful.

My thanks also go to Habyb 'Umar b. Hafez, who was my host in Tarim, Yemen, and at whose feet I studied a number of classics on spirituality and ethics.

I also acknowledge my indebtedness to Dr. Tareq Suwaidan, whose Arabic language lectures on the biography of the Prophet Muhammad, got me first deeply drawn not only to this great story, but also to the original texts which have transmitted it from generation to generation for nearly one thousand five hundred years.

I also thank the people who significantly contributed in one way or the other to this work. These include Sheikh Mustafa al-Hamadani, my Kenyan friends (Ahmed and Muhsin), Hajra Meeks, Professor Ismail Sesay in Niger, Professor Taymiya R Zaman, and Khaled Hussein.

I am also grateful to Fahim Munshi who did the final edits and formatting of the material for this book, and the deans of the College of Arts and Sciences of the University of San Francisco for providing funding for the project.

I address very special thanks to my wife, Fatima Maju, for her invaluable suggestions and unfailing support.

In the next section of this book a brief summary of the life of Prophet Muhammad is presented in order to serve as a useful introduction for some readers.

I hope that the reader will, in reading this work, gain more intimate access into the life of Islam's Prophet, as well as appreciate the book for the literary and aesthetic quality of its narratives.

San Francisco   Ahmed Bangura
July 2018

Prophet Muhammad
– A Brief Biographical Note

Muhammad was born to the Quraish tribe of Makkah, in Arabia, in 54 B.H. (571 AD). He lost his father before he was born. The Arabs of the time wanted their children to spend their early childhood in the desert, where they would learn pure Arabic and cultivate original virtues of the Arabs, such as bravery and generosity.

Muhammad, the child, was thus given to a Bedouin wet-nurse named Halima, who raised him in the desert for nearly four years before returning him to his mother, Amina. Amina died when Muhammad was only six years old. The orphaned boy then moved in with his grandfather, Abdul Muttalib, who loved him more than his own sons. Abdul Mutalib died when Muhammad was eight years old.

Muhammad then came under the care of his uncle, Abu Talib. Abu Talib was so poor that Muhammad took it upon himself at a very early age to raise sheep and goats in order to help his uncle. At the age of twelve, Muhammad accompanied his uncle on a trading trip to Shams (today's Palestine, Jordan and Syria). The adolescent Muhammad developed a talent for business, but what struck most people about him were his impeccable honesty, uprightness, and generosity.

Becoming independent through business, Muhammad sought to relieve his poor uncle by volunteering to raise one of his children, Ali.

His reputation caught the attention of an aristocratic businesswoman in

Makkah, Khadija Bint Khuwailid, a widow who had been married twice. She hired Muhammad for a business trip to Sham in the company of her servant, Maisara. When he returned from the trip, Maisara related to Khadija the noble characteristics he observed in Muhammad during their journey. His character and the unusually high profits of the business trip moved Khadija to propose marriage to Muhammad. Muhammad accepted, and at age twenty-five became the husband of forty-year old Khadija. Theirs was a marriage of love and compassion. They had five daughters and two sons, both sons dying in infancy.

At the age of forty, or shortly before that, Muhammad started to take periodic retreats in a cave on a hill facing Makkah. During those retreats, he worshipped God as he understood him at the time and contemplated life's meaning. He could not relate to the polytheistic culture of his people, who had deviated from the monotheism left by the Prophet Abraham (Ibrahim).

The Arabs had no less than three hundred and sixty gods in the Ka'aba, the cube-shaped building, which according to tradition, had been erected by Adam as God's first temple on earth and restored by Abraham (Ibrahim) and his son, Ishmael (Ismail).

During times of seclusion, Muhammad would retreat to the mountain cave of Hira facing Makkah. There, he would worship God in his own untutored ways. It was upon one such occasion that the Angel Gabriel unexpectedly appeared to him, and announced to him that he [Muhammad]—had been chosen by God to be His Last Messenger and the Seal of all the Prophets. The message he was ordered to convey is *Tawhid*—the pure monotheism taught by all prophets before him, who also preached brotherhood and the essential equality of all humans before God.

The Message presented a challenge to the privileges enjoyed by the Quraish tribe of Makkah—the custodians and patrons of the Ka'aba. It opposed many of the Arab ways, including their intractable tribalism and treatment of women and slaves.

The Prophet's fledgling following initially consisted mainly of slaves and the socially underprivileged. His followers faced great persecution. The suffering they endured in Makkah intensified after the deaths of Muhammad's uncle and protector, Abu Talib, and his wife and supporter, Khadija. These persecutions led to two migrations (hijra): the first to Abyssinia, then ruled by a just Christian king, and the second to Yathrib , an oasis town some two hundred miles from Makkah, and which would later be called *Madinat Arrassul* (The city of the Prophet). It is in Yathrib that the Muslims would for the first time be able to practice their religion openly without fear of persecution. Muhammad was invited by leading inhabitants of the town to immigrate with his followers and mediate between the town's clans in their unceasing wars and disputes.

The Muslims who migrated from Makkah will forever be called *Muhajiroon* (immigrants) and their hosts in Madinah the *Ansar* (Helpers). The Prophet quickly established the *Muwakha*, by which each Ansar would be paired with a Muhajir (one immigrant) as his special host and spiritual brother. He also dictated the Charter of Madinah, which established the laws and principles binding the members of this religiously pluralistic and multi-clan town into one community. Some of the clans were Jewish, either Arab converts or ethnic Jews who had migrated there a long while back.

While in Madinah, the Muslims received divine permission for the first time to engage in war for self-defense or in order to remove all threats to the new community's survival and growth (during their thirteen years in Makkah, Muslims had not been allowed to fight even in these circumstances).

It was also while in Madinah that the Prophet Muhammad married more wives, most of them divorced women or widows of his companions.

The Muslims fought many battles against their enemies, especially the Quraish of Makkah, many of whom were family members. The greatest of these battles were at Badr, where the Muslims won and at Uhud, where the Muslims lost.

Over the ensuing years, there were many other skirmishes and battles, continuing until the signing of the Treaty of Hudaibiya.

One thousand Muslims were present at the signing of the treaty between the Muslims and their Meccan opponents. The treaty brokered a few years of peace with the Meccans, which the Muslims used well for the preaching of the message of Islam throughout the Arabian Peninsula and beyond. After two years, the community counted ten thousand able-bodied men.

During this period, the Prophet sent letters to the rulers of distant places such as Persia, Byzantium and Egypt, inviting them to Islam. He even sent a delegation to China. Also during this time, individuals and groups came to Madinah to visit the Prophet. Some of them were new Muslims, and some would embrace Islam during their meeting with the Prophet.

The breaking of the truce by a party in Makkah led to the Prophet's decision to march on Makkah, and take the city by force, if necessary. Confronted by overwhelming numbers of Muslims, the Meccans surrendered. Triumphant, the Prophet led his army into the city with his head bowed in humility. He forgave old enemies and granted them amnesty.

After destroying the idols in the Ka'aba, the Prophet asked his companion and dear friend Bilal, a former slave of Abyssinian descent, to climb the sacred sanctuary, and to make for the first time the public call to prayer in Makkah.

As Makkah was the center of Arabia's religious life before Islam, soon thereafter, the rest of Arabia would enter the fold of Islam. The Prophet's mission of implanting monotheism in Arabia was fulfilled during his lifetime.

Two years after the opening of Makkah, Prophet Muhammad made his farewell pilgrimage (Hajj), accompanied by approximately one hundred thousand followers. He delivered his famous "Farewell Sermon" on Mount Arafat during this pilgrimage. The sermon stressed the fundamentals of the faith: the worship of one God, and the need for dignity and grace in man's treatment of his fellow man.

Following the pilgrimage, the Prophet returned to live in Madinah. He continued to receive revelation through the angel Gabriel until God took his soul in the eleventh year of his migration. He left the Muslims the Qur'an, which God had revealed to him progressively during his twenty-three year ministry, and the Sunna, his own personal example, as sources of guidance. He was buried in the room of 'A'isha, one of his wives, where he spent his final days.

He was sixty-three years old.

Chapter One

The Meccan Period

BABY MUHAMMAD NEEDS A WET-NURSE

'Abdullah, b. Ja'afar b. Abu Talib narrates that Halima Bint Abu Dhuaib of Banu Sa'ad clan, who would become the wet nurse of the Prophet Muhammad, (peace be upon him) used to say that she left her country with her husband and small child, whom she was nursing. She was in the company of women of the Banu Sa'ad b. Bakr clan. She traveled in the hope of getting a baby she would wet-nurse. She said, "It was a year of drought and famine, which left us with nothing

I rode out on a white jenny. We had with us an old camel, which did not give any milk. By God, not even a drop of milk would come from the she-camel. And we could not sleep at night, because our baby, who was with us, kept crying out of hunger. There was not enough milk in my breast to satisfy him, and the she-camel had no milk we could feed him. We were hoping for rain and relief.

So I rode my jenny until it became slow and delayed us. This caused much difficulty for her, and loss of weight. At length we reached Makkah to look for babies for wet-nursing. By God, Baby Muhammad was presented to each woman among us, but every single one of them turned him down when it was said: "He is an orphan." This is only because we were expecting a recompense from the baby's father. So we said, 'An orphan. What can his mother or grandfather possibly do?' We therefore rejected him. Finally, all the women who traveled with me found a suckling, except for me.

As we were about to leave, I told my husband, 'By God, I would hate to go back along with my fellow women without taking a suckling. By God, I will go to that orphan and take him.' He said, 'You will not be blamed for doing so. Perhaps God shall grant us blessings through him.'"

She said, "So I went and took him. And by God, I did not take him except because I had no alternative. When I took him, I brought him to my ride, placed him on my lap, and had him face my breasts. He drank as much as he wanted of my milk, until he was satisfied, and his brother (his milk-sibling) drank with him until he was satisfied. Then he slept. We had not slept with him before this time. My companion attempted to milk our she-camel. And behold he found her full of milk. He milked her, and both of us drank together, until we had our fill and spent the best of nights.

My husband said to me when we got up in the morning, 'By God, Halima, I see that you have acquired a blessed child.' I said, 'By God, I hope so.' Then we left, and I rode my jenny, and carried him with me on it.

And behold, my jenny was moving so fast that the other donkeys could not keep up with her. My fellow travelers said, 'O daughter of Dhuaib! What is the matter? Slow down!' Is this the same jenny that you had come with?' I said, 'Yes, By God it is indeed the same one.' They said: 'By God, there is something surely special about it.'"

She said, "Then we reached the territory of Banu Sa'ad, and I did not know a land of the lands of God more afflicted by bareness than it. But my sheep would go out to graze and return full of milk. We would milk them and drink. And no one had a sheep with a drop of milk, nor could they find any in the udders.

The sedentary dwellers of our country started to tell their shepherds: 'Come on, have your sheep graze where the shepherd of Bint Abu Dhuaib takes the sheep for grazing.' But their animals would return home hungry, and without a drop of milk. My sheep would return satiated and full of milk; and we continued to see blessings and increase in our provision from God's bounty until he (the baby) became two years old.

He was growing like no other child did. By God, by the time he was two he had become very sturdy."

She said, "We took him back to his mother, but with the strong desire to have him continue to stay with us, because of the great blessings that came from having him. We spoke to his mother, and I said to her, 'If only you could leave your son with me until he becomes strong, for I fear that he might catch the plague of Makkah.' We kept imploring until she allowed us to take him back with us."

KHADIJA PROPOSES MARRIAGE

Ibn Sa'ad relates that Nafisa Bint Muniya said: "Khadija Bint Khuwailid was a resolute and tough noble woman. In addition, God had adorned her with great goodness and generosity. She was a Quraish woman of the most noble lineage, great honor, and was the wealthiest among Quraish. All the men of her community were eager to marry her if only they could. They spent much money trying to win her!

(But) she sent me to Muhammad as a secret agent after he returned from her commercial errand in Sham. I said: 'Muhammad, what is keeping you from getting married?' He said, 'I do not have the means for marriage.' I said, 'What if that is taken care of, and you are offered to marry a woman of beauty, wealth, nobility, and compatibility, would you accept?' He said, 'Who is she then?' I said, 'Khadija.' He said, 'How do I go about this?' I said, 'Leave everything up to me.' He said, 'Then I would.'"

GABRIEL BRINGS DOWN THE REVELATION

Aisha, Mother of the believers, relates, "The forerunners of the revelation assumed the form of true dreams. He (the Prophet) never saw a vision except that it was as one sees the appearance of the horizon at daybreak. Then solitude became dear to him and he would go to the cave, Hira, to engage in *Tahannuth*–that was worship in a given number of nights–before returning to his family to get more provisions. He would then return to Khadija to prepare for a similar stay.

At length, the Truth (the angel Gabriel) came to him while in the cave of Hira. The angel appeared to him and said: 'Recite!' He (the Prophet) said: 'I cannot recite.' Then he (the Prophet) related: 'He grabbed me and squeezed me very hard, and then loosened the grip and said: 'Recite!' 'I cannot recite,' I said. For a second time he squeezed me until I gasped for breath, then released me and said: 'Recite!' I said, 'I cannot recite.' He squeezed me for the third time and then let me go and said: *Recite! In the name of your Lord, who has created, created man from a clot of sensitive blood. Recite! And your Lord is most generous."* (96: 1-3)

The Prophet (pbuh) returned home with his heart beating fast. He went to Khadija Bint Khuwailid and said: 'Cover me. Cover me.' They covered him until he calmed down. Then he related the incident: 'I was afraid for my life.' She (Khadija) said: 'God will never disgrace you. You unite kin, you bear the burden of the weak, you help the poor and the needy, and you are hospitable to guests and endure hardship in the name of truth.'

She set out with the Prophet to her cousin, Waraqa b. Nawfal b. Asad b. Abdul-Uzza, who had embraced Christianity in the pre-Islamic period and used to write the writing with Hebrew letters. He used to write from the Gospel in Hebrew as much as God wished him to write. He was a blind old man. Khadija said, 'My cousin! Listen to your nephew!' Waraqa said, 'My cousin! What did you see?' He (the Prophet) told him what had happened to him. Waraqa said to him: 'This is Namus (the angel who transmits divine revelation) that God had sent to Moses. I wish I were younger.

I wish I could live longer up to the time when your people will expel you.' The Messenger of God asked, 'Will they drive me out?' He said: 'Yes. No one has ever come with something like what you have brought except that he is treated with hostility. If I should be alive till that day, then I would support you resolutely.' A few days later, Waraqa died and the revelation subsided.

KHADIJA SEEKS TO VERIFY IF MUHAMMAD'S UNIQUE VISITOR IS TRULY THE ANGEL GABRIEL

Ibn Hisham relates that Khadija asked the Messenger of God, "Cousin, can you tell me when this companion of yours, who keeps coming to you, comes the next time?" He said, "Yes." She said, "So when he comes let me know.'

Then the Angel Gabriel arrived as usual, and the Messenger of God said to Khadija, "O Khadija! Here comes Gabriel; he is here." She said, "Get up, O cousin, and sit on my left thigh." The Messenger of God got up and sat on it. She said, "Do you see him (now)?" He said, "Yes." She said, "Then move over and sit on my right thigh." The Messenger of God moved over and sat on her right thigh. She said, "Do you see him (now)?" He said, "Yes." She said, "Move over and sit on my lap." The Messenger of God moved over and sat on her lap. She said, "Do you see him?" He said, "Yes." She then took off her headscarf, while the Prophet still sat on her lap. And she asked him, "Do you see him (now)?" He said, "No." She said, "O cousin, be resolute, and rejoice. For verily this is an angel. This is not the devil."

THE PROPHET WEEPS

Ibn Ishaq narrates: When Quraish said what they said to Abu Talib, he (Abu Talib) sent for the Messenger of God. He said to him (upon his arrival), "O my nephew, your people have come to me and said so and so. Please spare me and yourself, and do not put on me a burden greater than I can bear.

The Messenger of God thought that his uncle was ready to forsake him and give him up (to his Meccan enemies), that he had become tired of helping him and standing by him.

The Messenger of God said, "O Uncle, by God if they put the sun in my right hand and the moon in my left hand on the condition that I abandon my mission before God grants it victory, or else I perish in its cause, I would not accept." The tears started rolling down his cheeks, and he wept. He then got up. And when he turned his back (to leave), Abu Talib called him back, saying, "Come here, my nephew." The Messenger of God came toward him. Then Abu Talib said, "My nephew, go! By God, never will I give you up for anything in the world."

AMRU B. ABASA AL-SULAMI APPROACHES THE PROPHET

Amru b. Abasa al-Sulami said, "Before Islam, I believed the people were wrong and deluded, and what they worshipped were mere idols.

Then I heard about a man in Makkah, who was giving news of (the other world). So I sat on my camel to go and meet with him. I discovered the Messenger of God operating in secrecy, while his people who were opposed to him had the upper hand. So I entered Makkah discretely until I came into his presence (and started to talk to him): "Who are you?"

"I am a prophet."

"And what's a prophet?"

"God has sent me."

"And what has God sent you with?"

"He has sent me to strengthen family ties, to call for the breaking of idols, and to teach the affirmation of God's absolute oneness."

"And who else is with you in this new faith?" I asked.

"Two: a free man and a slave," he replied. (Among the believers at that time were Abu Bakr and Bilal).

"Well, I will follow you."

"I don't think you have the strength for it at this time." He told me. "Don't you see my situation and the situation of the people? For now, return to your own people until you hear news of my prevailing. Then you should come to (join) me."

DIMAD SEEKS TO HEAL THE PROPHET

It is related on the authority of Ibn Abbas that Dimad traveled to Makkah. He heard the foolish among the people of Makkah saying, "Truly Muhammad is mad." Dimad said, "If I saw this man, perhaps God might cure him through me." Then he met him and said, "O Muhammad, God cures through me whom He wills. May I try?"

The Messenger of God said, "All praise and thanks are for God. We praise Him, and we seek His help. Whoever God guides none can misguide. And whoever He lets to go astray, no one can guide. And I bear witness that there is no divinity other than God, the One. He has no partners. And that Muhammad is his servant and envoy."

Dimad said, "Please repeat these words of yours for me."

The Messenger of God repeated them thrice.

Dimad said, "I have heard the words of fortunetellers, and the words of magicians, and the words of poets. But I have never heard anything like these words of yours. This is the zenith of the sublime." Dimad then said, "Give me your hand, so that I take the pledge of faith in Islam." He made his pledge. Then the Messenger of God asked, "And on behalf of your people?" Dimad replied, "And on behalf of my people."

ABU LAHAB FRUSTRATES HIS NEPHEW'S OUTREACH EFFORTS

Rabi'a b. Abbad al-Daili said: "I was a young man accompanying my father. I watched the Messenger of God as he walked through the quarters of Arab tribes (in Mina). Behind him was a cross-eyed man with a beaming face, and with a long lock of hair. The Messenger of God would stop (at each tribe's encampment) and say, 'O such and such tribe, I am God's Messenger to you. I beseech you to worship God, and not to ascribe partners to him. Believe me and support me, so that I fulfill the mission for which I was sent.' As soon as he finished his address, the one walking behind him would say, 'O tribe such and such: This man is asking you to abandon al-Lat and al-Uzza (their two principal idols) and to forsake your allies from the Jinn, for the sake of what he has brought by way of innovation and misguidance. Do not listen to him! Do not follow him!' I asked my father, 'Who is this?' He said, 'Abu Lahab, his uncle.'

THE PROPHET IS THROTTLED

'Urwa b. al-Zubair narrated: "I asked 'Abdullah b. 'Amr b. al-'As to tell me of the worst thing that the pagans did to the Prophet (PBUH). He said: 'While the Prophet (PBUH) was praying in Al-Hjir of the Ka'aba, Uqba b. Abu Mu'ait came and put his garment around the Prophet's neck and throttled him violently. Abu Bakr came and caught him by his shoulder and pushed him away from the Prophet, and said 'Do you want to kill a man, just because he says My Lord is God?'"

AL-TUFAYL B. AMRU AL-DAUSI, THE POET, ASSESSES THE PROPHET

Ibn Ishaq relates that al-Tufayl b. Amru al-Dausi, a noble poet with a sharp intellect, said that he traveled to Makkah while the Messenger of God was there, and men from Quraish approached him. They said to him: "You have come to our country, and that man—this one right here—has sown dissension in our assemblies and brought discord to our affairs. His speech is like that of a magician. By it, he separates a man from his brother and he separates a man from his wife. We truly fear for you and your people that what happened to us will befall you. So do not talk to him and do not listen to him!"

Al-Tufayl said: "By God, they were so persistent that I determined not to hear anything from him and not to speak to him to the extent that I put cotton in my ears as I made my way to the Mosque. This was to make sure that nothing of what he said would reach my ears. So I went to the Mosque, and behold, the Messenger of God was standing in prayer by the Ka'aba. So I stood close to him, and God willed that I heard some of what he said. I heard beautiful words. So I said to myself, 'By God, I am an intelligent and discerning poet. I can tell beauty from ugliness. What then prevents me from listening to what this man is saying? If what he says is beautiful, I will accept it; and if ugly, I will reject it.' So I stayed around until the Messenger of God left for his home, and I followed him. When he entered his house I followed him in and said, 'O Muhammad, your people have told me this and that. They warned me so much about you that out of fear, I blocked my ears with cotton lest I should hear your words. Then God would have it in no other way except that I should hear them. So I heard some beautiful words. Please tell me, what are you calling for?'

The Messenger of God spoke to me about Islam and recited the Qur'an. By God, I had never before heard anything more beautiful than it and no message fairer than it. I embraced Islam, and I took the oath of allegiance to the Truth."

FLIGHT TO ABYSSINIA (ETHIOPIA) FOR REFUGE

Ibn Ishaq relates: "The Messenger of God saw the great suffering of his followers, which he was spared by divine intervention and by the protection of his uncle. Not being able to protect them himself, he said to them, 'Flee to Abyssinia, whose king (a Christian) allows no one to be treated unjustly in his land. It is a land of truth. Stay there until God changes your condition

14

for the better.' At that point some of the Muslims among the companions of the Messenger of God fled to the land of Abyssinia out of fear of further tribulation. This was also their flight toward God and for the protection of their faith. This was the first hijra (migration) in Islam."

KHADIJA'S MEMORY WILL LINGER ON

'A'isha said: "I was not jealous of any woman as much as I was of Khadija. She had passed away before he (the Prophet) married me. This is because of the way he used to mention and remember her.

For example, God had asked him to give her the glad tidings of a mansion of hollowed pearls in Paradise. Whenever he slaughtered a goat, he would give a sufficient portion of it as a gift to her former close friends."

KHADIJAH'S OLD FRIEND RECEIVES SPECIAL TREATMENT

'A'isha narrates: "An old lady once came to the Prophet. He said, 'How are you? How are you doing? How have you been since those days?' She said, 'O Messenger of God, for whose sake I can sacrifice my father and mother, I am doing well.' When she left, I said, 'You received this old woman with so much warmth!' He said, 'O 'A'isha, she used to visit us during the days of Khadija. Honoring relationships is part of faith.'"

KHADIJA, THE UNIQUE

'A'isha relates: "The Prophet always praised Khadija profusely whenever he mentioned her. One day I became jealous and said, 'You mention that terribly old woman so often. God has substituted her with someone better than her.' He said, 'God has not substituted her with someone better than her. She believed in me, when others disbelieved in me. She thought me truthful, while others claimed that I was a liar. And she comforted me with her wealth, while others were keen on depriving me. God blessed me to have children by her, while he deprived me such a blessing with other women."

THE DEATH OF A PROTECTOR

Ibn Ishaq wrote: "When Abu Talib died, Quraish inflicted pain on the Messenger of God, in ways they could not have dared while Abu Talib was alive. Even a low character from Quraish confronted him and poured dust on his head. The Messenger of God entered his house with the dirt on his head. One of his daughters stood up to wash the dirt off, while crying. The Messenger of God said to her, 'Don't cry, my little girl. God will protect your father.'"

THE PROPHET PRAYS AFTER BANU THAQIF HURT AND TORTURED HIM

'Abdullah b. Jaafar said: "When Abu Talib died, the Prophet traveled to Taif on foot in order to call them (the people of Taif) to Islam. They did not heed his call. He therefore left and came to the shade provided by a tree, and did two units of prayer (rakaa). He then supplicated:

'O God, I complain to you of the feebleness of my ability, the scarcity of my means, and my humiliation before the people.

You are the source of all mercy, the Lord of the weak, and my Lord.

With whom shall you entrust my care? Shall you entrust it with an enemy who would angrily frown at me, or with the unsympathetic relative you have given control of my affair?

If you are not angry with me, nothing else matters. But I stand in greater need of your compassionate Grace.

I seek protection in the light of Your countenance, on whose account all darkness gives way to light, and all affairs of the world and the Hereafter are rectified.

This is better for me than that your anger descend upon me, or that your displeasure should overwhelm me.

I will seek to please you until you show your pleasure.

There is no power, and no strength except in you (and through you).

BANU THAQIF'S REJECTION MARKS
THE LOWEST POINT IN THE PROPHET'S MISSION

'A'isha (once) asked the Prophet, "Has any day been harder on you than the Day of Uhud (When the Muslins suffered a crushing defeat, and the Prophet was severely wounded, and for a while thought to have been killed)?"

The Prophet replied, "I have suffered a great deal at the hands of your people, but the worst I have been through was on the Day of al-Aqabah. I presented myself to Abd Yalil b. Abd Kullal, but he refused to grant me what I asked for. I felt devastated and left him. In that state I arrived at Qarn al-Tha'alib.

When I raised my eyes to the sky, I saw a cloud over me. Then I looked. And behold, there was the Angel Gabriel in the cloud. He addressed me, saying, 'God has heard your people's response to you and their words, and He has sent you the angel in charge of the mountains, ready to do as you command.' The angel of the mountains called and greeted me, and he said, 'O Muhammad, God has heard the words of your people to you, and I am the angel of the mountains. Your Lord has sent me to you; so that you can command me as you wish. If you want, I shall bring the mountains over their heads.'

I said, 'By no means.' I hoped that God would bring forth from their loins descendants who would worship God alone and associate no partners with him.'"

~

Chapter Two

Life in Madinah and Opening of Makkah

THE BRIGHTEST DAY OF MADINAH

Anas, b. Malik said: "I was rushing among the young boys, who were shouting, 'Muhammad has arrived.' I kept walking about, but I saw nothing. Finally, the Messenger of God arrived with his companion, Abu Bakr. We were in a neighborhood of Madinah. Then a man of the people of Madinah sent us to go and grant them (the Prophet and Abu Bakr) leave to enter the city on behalf of the people of Madinah. Around five hundred of the Ansar (residents of Madinah) welcomed them (the Prophet and Abu Bakr). They all headed toward them until they reached them. The Ansar said, 'Welcome, we pledge to you our protection and obedience.'

The Messenger of God and his companion then moved into the crowd, and the people of Madinah came out. Even the old women were up on the rooftops to watch them. They asked, 'Which of them is the one?'

We had never seen a scene like this before. I saw him the day he came to us, and the day he passed away. I have never seen two days like them."

In another narration, Anas said: "Abu Bakr rode behind the Messenger of God (on the same camel) between Makkah and Madinah. Before this, Abu Bakr used to travel to Sham (Syria), and so he was known, but the Messenger of God was not known. People they passed by would ask, 'O Abu Bakr, who is this fellow riding with you?'

He would reply, 'He is showing me the way.'

When they got close to Madinah they sent for the Ansar, who came saying, 'We welcome you, and pledge to you our protection and obedience.'

I saw the day he entered Madinah, and I have never seen a more beautiful and brighter day than it. And I saw him the day he died, and I have not seen a more terrible and somber day than it."

EXCERPTS FROM THE PROPHET'S CHARTER OF MADINAH

In the name of God, the Most Merciful, the Most Beneficent.

This is a document drawn up by Muhammad (pbuh) the Prophet, to regulate affairs between the believers and Muslims of Quraish and of Yathrib and whoever joins them and participates in their Jihad. They are a single nation.

The Muhajiroon (immigrants) of the Quraish remain the same and bear responsibility for the blood money they incur. They pay for the release of their prisoners in a manner that is reasonable and fair among believers.

And 'Auf clan remains the same and bears responsibility for the blood money it incurs. Each group pays for the release of its prisoners, in accordance with what is reasonable and fair among believers.

And Banu Sa'ida clan remains the same and bears responsibility for the blood money it incurs. Each group pays for the release of its prisoners, in accordance with what is reasonable and fair among believers.

And Banu al-Harith clan remains the same and bears responsibility for the blood money it incurs. Each group pays for the release of its prisoners, in accordance with what is reasonable and fair among believers.

And Banu Gusham clan remains the same and bears responsibility for the blood money it incurs. Each group pays for the release of its prisoners, in accordance with what is reasonable and fair among believers.

And whoever among the Jews joins partners with us is entitled to equality in treatment and our assistance. They should not be oppressed. And no one shall help their enemies against them.

The peace and security of the believers is one and indivisible. No separate peace shall be made when believers are fighting in the way of God. Conditions must be fair and equitable to all.

It is incumbent on the believers to avenge the blood of one another shed in the way of God.

Whoever is convicted of unjustly killing a believer will be subjected to retaliation unless the next of kin (of the murdered person) is satisfied (with blood-money).

The believers shall be against him as one man, and they are obligated to take action against him.

No believer who signs on to this document and believes in God and the last day may give support or shelter to a criminal. Whoever does that, will incur God's curse and His anger on the Day of Judgment and no repentance or compensation will be received from him.

The Jews shall share expenses with the Muslims as long as they are at war (with others).

And the Jews of Banu 'Auf clan are one nation with the believers (Muslims). The Jews are entitled to their religion and alliances and their lives, just as the Muslims are entitled to their religion and alliances and lives, except for the one who does wrong and oppresses others. Such a person only brings to ruin himself and his household.

And the Jews of Banu al-Najar clan are like the Jews of the 'Auf clan. And the Jews of Banu Sa'ida clan are like the Jews of the 'Auf clan.

And the Jews of Banu Jusham clan are like the Jews of the 'Auf clan.

And the Jews of Banu al-Aws clan are like the Jews of the 'Auf clan.

The Jews shall bear their own expenses, and the Muslims shall bear their own expenses. Between them is the pledge of mutual assistance when any signatory to this document is attacked. And between them also is the pledge of mutual advice and righteousness, except in ways that are iniquitous, for no one shall be considered a wrongdoer on account of the actions of his ally.

And assistance should go to the one who has been wronged.

And the Jews share expenses with the believers as long as they are at war (with an outside force).

And Yathrib shall remain inviolable to the signatories of this document.

And everyone's neighbor is as precious as oneself, except in cases of harm and wrongdoing.

This document will not protect the oppressor and sinner. Whoever chooses to stay (in Madinah) is safe, and whoever chooses to leave is safe, except for one who does wrong and is oppressive. For God grants sanctuary to those who fulfill their pledges and are God conscious. And so it is with Muhammad, the messenger of God.

This is a document prepared by the Messenger of God to define the relationship between him and the Jews.

THE PLOT OF SAFWAN AND ʿUMAYR AFTER THE BATTLE OF BADR

ʿUmayr b. Wahb al-Jumahiy sat for a short while with Safwan b. Umayya to speak about the Quraish victims of the battle of Badr by the Hijr spot (close to the Ka'aba). Umayr was one of those who tormented the Messenger of God and his companions and caused them much hardship while they were in Makkah. His son, Wahab b. ʿUmayr, was among the prisoners of Badr. They remembered the people of al-Qalib and their misfortunes ("al-Qalib" refers to the grave in which the Muslims buried the Meccan dead of Badr).

Safwan said, "By God, there is no good in living after them?" ʿUmayr b. Wahab said, "That is true, by God had it not been for the fact that I have a debt which I cannot repay and a family whose suffering I fear if I should die, I would have gone to Mohammad and killed him."

"After all, I have a very good reason to do so; they (Muslims of Madinah) hold my son prisoner." Safwan saw the opportunity and said, "I will take care of your debt, and your family will be just like mine. They will be in need of nothing that I cannot take care of. 'Umayr said, "Keep this affair of mine and yours a secret." Safwan said, "I will."

'Umayr asked for his sword, had it sharpened and poisoned, and set out for Madinah.

In Madinah, 'Umar b. al-Khattab was sitting with a group of Muslims, talking about the Day of Badr, how God had honored them on that day, and what he had shown them regarding their enemies. Suddenly he saw 'Umayr b. Wahab, who had dismounted and tied his camel at the doorstep of the Masjid. He had his sword in combat readiness.

'Umar said, "This dog, this enemy of God, 'Umayr b. Wahab, has undoubtedly come intending evil. He was the one who stirred up trouble and guessed at our numbers for the benefit of our enemies on the day of Badr." Immediately, 'Umar went to the Prophet and said, "O Prophet of God, 'Umayr b Wahab, God's enemy, has just arrived carrying his sword." The Prophet said, "Let him in."

'Umar went to him, took the belt on which he hung his sword, put it around his neck, and let him through. He also said to the Ansar who were with him, "Come in and sit with the Prophet. Be on your guard against this dog; he is not to be trusted." Then 'Umar brought 'Umayr to the Prophet, pulling him with the belt of his sword around his neck. The prophet said: "Release him, O 'Umar!, and 'Umayr, come closer." He got closer and said, "Happy Morning," which was the greeting of the people before the time of Islam. The Prophet of God said, "God has blessed us with a greeting that is better than your greeting, O 'Umayr, Assalam, which is the greeting of the people of paradise."

'Umayr said, "By God, O Muhammad, I have heard that only recently."

The Prophet said, "What brought you here?"

He said, "I came for the prisoner whom you are holding. Treat him well."

He said, "What about the sword around your neck?"

He said, "May God damn these swords! What good have they brought us?"

He said, "Tell me the truth, what is the purpose of your coming?"

He said, "I only came for that (as mentioned above)."

He said, "Not so; you and Safwan b. Umayyah sat at the Hijr and spoke about the losses of Quraish (at Badr) and the people of al-Qalib. You said to him, 'Had it not been for my debts and my children, I would have gone to kill Muhammad.'"

"Safwan then took it upon himself to pay your debts and take care of your children in return for your killing me. But God has placed a wall between you and your purpose."

'Umayr said, "I testify that you are the Messenger of God. We used to belie what you relayed to us from the heavens, and what came to you by way of revelation, O Messenger of God. Only Safwan and myself witnessed this plot. I have no doubt that only God could have informed you about it. I praise and thank God, who has guided me to Islam and made me travel this path." He then made the Testimony of Truth (the shahada), and the Messenger of God said, "Teach your brother about his religion, how to recite the Qur'an, and free his prisoner."

HELPING AN UNWANTED HUSBAND

Ibn 'Abbas said, "The husband of Buraira was a slave called Mughith–(as I speak now) it is as if I can see him circling around her weeping (in another narration, 'it's as if I can see him following in the alleys of Madinah'), his tears streaming on his beard." So the Prophet said to Abbas, "Aren't you amazed at Mughith's (desperate) love for Buraira, and at Buraira's strong dislike for Mughith? " So the Prophet said to her, "I wish you could go back to him, for he is the father of your son." She replied, "O Messenger of God, are you ordering me to?" He replied, "No, I am only interceding." She said, "Then, I have no need of him."

HABITS AT HOME

Al-Aswad b. Yazid said, "I asked 'A'isha, 'What did the Prophet, may God bless him and grant him peace, used to do in his house?' She said, 'He would be at the service of his family. When it was time for the prayer, he would go out to the prayer.'"

SEEKING PERMISSION FOR AN EXTRA GUEST

Abu Mas'ud al-Ansari said: "A man of the Ansar called Abu Shu'ayb had a slave who was a butcher. He came to the Prophet, peace be upon him, while he was with his companions, and noticed hunger on the face of the Prophet (pbuh). He went to his slave, the butcher, and said, 'Prepare enough food for five. Perhaps I will invite the Prophet, may God bless him and grant him peace, as one of five guests. Abu Shu'ayab prepared a little bit of food and went to the Prophet (pbuh) to invite him. A man tagged along. The Prophet (pbuh) said, 'This man has followed us. Will you give him permission?' He let him in."

A TRYING DAY FOR ABU HURAIRA

Mujahid related that Abu Huraira said: "By God. There is no god but Him, I used to lie on my stomach on the ground out of hunger, and I used to tie a stone to my belly because of hunger. One day, I sat by a road by which people went out. Abu Bakr passed by, and I asked him about a verse of the Book of God, and I only asked him so that he would satisfy my hunger. He passed by and did not do it. Then 'Umar passed by and I asked him about a

24

verse of the Book of God, and I only asked him so that he would satisfy my hunger. He passed by and did not do it. Then Abu'l-Qasim (the Prophet [pbuh]), passed by and he smiled when he saw me and recognized what was inside of me and what was in my face. He said, 'Abu Hirr!' I answered, 'At your service, Messenger of God!' He said, 'Come along.' He went, and I followed him. He went inside, and I asked permission to enter, and he gave me permission. He entered and found some milk in a bowl and said, 'Where is this milk from?' They said, 'It was given to you by so-and-so (either a man or a woman).' He said, 'Abu Hirr!' I answered, 'At your service, Messenger of God!' He said, 'Go and invite the people of the Suffa for me.' The people of the Suffa were the guests of Islam who had no family, property, or anything to resort to. When a charitable donation came, he used to send it to them and not take any of it. When a gift came to him, he would send some and take some and let them share in it. That annoyed me, and I said to myself, 'What good will this milk be among the people of the Suffa?' I thought that I was more entitled to have a drink of this milk to strengthen myself thereby, but then he came and ordered me to give it to them, and I wondered if I would get any of this milk. But God and His Messenger, may God bless him and grant him peace, must be obeyed.

"I went to the people of the Suffa and invited them, and they accepted. They asked permission to enter, and he gave them permission. They took their seats in the house, and he said, 'Abu Hirr!' I answered, 'At your service, Messenger of God!' He said, 'Take it and give it to them.' I took the bowel and gave it to a man who drank his fill and returned the bowl to me. I gave it to another man who drank his fill and returned the bowl to me. Another drank until he was full and returned the bowl to me. I reached the Prophet, may God bless him and grant him peace, after all the group had drunk their fill. He took the bowl and put it in his hand. Then he looked at me and smiled and said, 'Abu Hirr!' I answered, 'At your service, Messenger of God!' He said, 'You and I remain.' I said, 'You spoke the truth, Messenger of God.' He said, 'Sit and drink.' I sat and drank. He said, 'Drink.' So I drank. He continued to say 'Drink' until I said, 'No, by the One who sent you with the truth, I have no room for it!' He said, 'Give it to me.' I gave him the bowl and he praised God, said the name of God and drank the rest."

WHEN FAMILY GETS IN THE WAY: AN INTIMATE MOMENT

It is related that 'A'isha, the wife of the Prophet (pbuh), said: "We went out with the Messenger of God, may God bless him and grant him peace, on one of his journeys until, when we reached al-Bayda, or Dhat al-Jaysh, my necklace broke and the Messenger of God, may God bless him and grant him peace, stayed to look for it and everyone else stayed with him. There was no water there, so the people went to Abu Bakr al-Siddiq and said, 'Look what 'A'isha has done. She has caused the Messenger of God, may God bless him and grant him peace, and everyone else to halt at a place where there is no water for them, nor are they carrying any water with them!' Abu Bakr came and found that the Messenger of God, may God bless him and grant him peace, had gone to sleep with his head against my thigh. He said, 'You have held up the Messenger of God and everyone else in a place where there is no water, and they are not carrying any water with them!' He rebuked me saying what God wished him to say and started to poke me in the side with his hand, and the only reason I did not move was that the Messenger of God, may God bless him and grant him peace, was against my thigh. At first light the Messenger of God, may God bless him and grant him peace, got up and found that there was no water. Then God sent down the verse of tayammum (dry ablution). So they did tayammum."

Usayd b. al-Hudayr said, 'Family of Abu Bakr, this is not the first blessing you have brought!'

26

'A'isha continued, "We made the camel I was on get up and found the necklace underneath it."

TOUGH 'UMAR IS AMAZED

Sa'ad b. Abi Waqqas related from his father: " 'Umar sought permission to enter the dwelling of the Messenger of God, while there were some women of Quraish with him and they were asking him to give them more financial support while raising their voices over the voice of the Prophet (pbuh). When 'Umar asked for permission to enter, they (the women) rushed to screen themselves. So 'Umar entered while the Messenger is laughing. 'Umar said, 'May God make you laugh, Messenger of God! Let my father and mother be sacrificed for you. The Messenger of God said, 'I am surprised at these (women), who were with me, but rushed to screen themselves as soon as they heard your voice.'

So 'Umar said, 'But you, Messenger of God, are more entitled to inspire awe in them.' Then he added, 'O enemies of yourselves, do you hold me and not the Messenger of God in awe?'

They said, 'Yes, you are harsher and more severe than the Messenger of God.' The Messenger of God said, 'O Ibn al-Khattab! By the One in whose hand my soul is, Shaytan (Satan) will not see you on a path except that he will (avoid you and) take a path different from your path.'"

GHAWRATH ATTEMPTS TO ASSASSINATE THE MESSENGER OF GOD

Jabir Ibn 'Abdullah reports: "A man called Ghawrath, from the tribe of Muharib, said to his people, the tribes of Ghatfan and Muharib, 'Should I kill Muhammad for you?' They replied, 'Yes, but how will you do it?' Ghawrath replied, 'I will take him unawares and kill him.'

He then went to the Prophet (pbuh) and found him sitting alone, his sword unsheathed. He said, "Muhammad, may I have a look at your sword?"

The Prophet (pbuh) said, 'Yes.' Then he took it and drew it out of its scabbard and started shaking it repeatedly and aiming it (at the Prophet [pbuh]). God kept deflecting it away. Ghawrath said, 'O Muhammad, don't you fear me?'

He said 'No, and what about you should I fear?' Ghawrath said, 'Don't you fear me, and I have the sword in my hand?' The Prophet (pbuh) said, 'I do not fear you. God will protect me from you.'

(In a version of the story in Imam Ahmed's Musnad, the following is added):

He then took aim at Muhammad, and God brought the sword into the possession of the Prophet (pbuh). God then Revealed the Verse.

"O you who have believed, remember God's favor upon you when a people desired (made a plan) to stretch out their hands against you but God held back their hands from you. Be conscious of God, and let those who believe place their reliance on God." (5:11)

Imam Ahmed added in his version of the hadith:

"The sword dropped from his hand, and the Messenger of God took it and said, 'Who will protect you from me?' He (Ghawrath) replied: 'Be the best man to overpower an opponent.' The Prophet (pbuh) said, 'Would you bear witness that there is no deity except God?' Ghawrath replied, 'No, but I pledge that I will never fight you, and I will never join any people who fight you.' Then he (the Prophe [pbuh]) let him go, and Ghawrath went to his people and said, 'I have come to you from the best of men.'"

WINNING RACES AND A LESSON OF HUMILITY

Humayd al-Tawil related that Anas said: "The Prophet (pbuh), may God bless him and grant him peace, had a she-camel called al-'Adba which could not be outrun in a race. A bedouin came on the youngish camel and outran it. That was difficult for the Muslims. They said, 'al-'Adba has been outrun.' The Messenger of God said, 'It is a right of God that nothing elevates itself in this world, except that He will bring it down.'"

A Wife's Support of her Poor Husband

Zainab, wife of 'Abdullah, relates, "I was in the mosque and saw the Prophet Muhammad (pbuh) telling women to give charity, even of their jewelry." Zainab was supporting 'Abdullah and many orphans in her care, so she told 'Abdullah to inquire from the Prophet (pbuh) whether her support of 'Abdullah and the orphans in her care could be counted as part of charity. 'Abdullah told her to go ask him herself.

So Zainab went to the Prophet (pbuh). She found a woman from the helpers, who had the same concern, at the door. At that point, Bilal passed by, and the two women asked him to ask the Prophet (pbuh) , on their behalf, whether a woman's support of her husband and orphans in her care counts as part of charity. They requested that Bilal not inform the prophet about them.

So. Bilal went and asked the question. The prophet asked him who the two women were, and Bilal mentioned Zainab's name. The prophet asked, "Which Zainab?" Bilal replied that it was the wife of 'Abdullah. The prophet said, "The answer is yes, and she will have two rewards: reward for taking care of relatives, and reward for charity."

Reasoning with One Bent on Fornication

Abu Umama said: "A young man came to the prophet and said, 'O Messenger of God, give me permission to fornicate!' People rushed forward and started to rebuke him and drive him away, saying 'Stop! Stop!' He (the Prophet [pbuh]) said, 'Bring him close to me!' So he came close and sat. He (the Prophet [pbuh]) asked, "Would you be pleased that it be done with your mother?'

The man replied, 'No, by God! May God sacrifice me for your sake!'

He (the Prophet [pbuh]) said, 'Nor do other people like that for their mothers.'

He (the Prophet) then said, 'Would you be pleased that it be done with your daughter?'

The young man replied, "No, by God! May God sacrifice me for your sake!'

He (the Prophet [pbuh]) said, 'Nor do other people like that for their daughters.' He (the Prophet [pbuh]) then said, 'Would you be pleased that it be done with your sister?'

The young man replied, "No, by God! May God sacrifice me for your sake!'

He (the Prophet [pbuh]) said, 'Nor do other people like that for their sisters.' He (the Prophet [pbuh]) then said, 'Would you be pleased that it be done with your paternal aunt?'

The young replied, "No, by God! May God sacrifice me for your sake!'

He (the Prophet [pbuh]) said, 'Nor do other people like that for their paternal aunts.'

He (the Prophet [pbuh]) then said, 'Would you be pleased that it be done with your maternal aunt?'

The young man replied, "No, by God! May God sacrifice me for your sake!'

He (the Prophet [pbuh]) said, 'Nor do other people like that for their maternal aunts.'

The Prophet (pbuh) then placed his hands on him and prayed, "O Lord, forgive his sin, purify his heart, and make him chaste. From that day on the young man never had an inclination toward anything (like fornication)."

ASMA'S NON-MUSLIM MOTHER VISITS

Ibn Hisham narrates on the authority of his father, who narrates that Asma, the daughter of Abu Bakr, said: "My mother traveled (from Makkah to Madinah) to see me, while she was a polytheist, and I asked the Messenger of God, 'O Messenger of God, my mother has come to me wanting something. Should I receive her well?' He replied, 'Yes, receive her well.'"

Shall I Show You a Woman of Paradise?

Ata b. Abu Rabah said that Ibn Abbass told him, "Shall I show you a woman of the people of Paradise?" Ata b. Abu Rabah said, "Please do!" Ibn Abbass said: "This black lady came to the Prophet (pbuh) and said, 'I have epileptic seizures, and my body becomes exposed. Please supplicate God on my behalf.' He (the Prophet [pbuh]) said, 'If you wish, endure patiently and you will have paradise, or if you wish, I will call on God to cure you.' She said, 'I will be patient, but supplicate God so that my body is not exposed (when I have seizures).' So he prayed for her."

The Prophet (pbuh) Consults His Companions on Strategy Regarding the Battle of Uhud

Ibn Ishaq relates that the Prophet (pbuh)said to his companions, "What do you think if you let them (the enemy from Makkah) remain wherever they decide to encamp? If they stay there, that would be the worst of places to stay. But if they decide to enter the city, we will fight them in it."

'Abdullah b. Ubayy b. Salul shared the Prophet's (pbuh) opinion that they should not go out to meet the enemy. And the Prophet (pbuh) disliked going out to meet them. Some of the Muslim men, who would be blessed with martyrdom on the Day of Uhud, and others who had missed participating in Badr said: "O Messenger of God, take us to meet our enemies. Let them not believe us to be cowards and weaklings!"

'Abdullah b. Ubayy b. Salul said: "O Messenger of God, stay in Madinah. Let us not go out to meet them. For by God, we have never left it to meet an enemy except that we were defeated, and (an enemy) has never entered it, except that we defeated him. So let them come. O Messenger of God, if they encamped outside they would be encamping in the worst of predicaments, and if they entered the men would fight them face to face while women and children would pelt them with stones from above, and if they retreat they would return demoralized, just as they came."

Those who wanted to meet the enemy persisted in making their case to the Messenger of God until the Messenger of God entered his house and put on his armor. It was on a Yaum al-Jumua'a (Friday) after the congregational prayers.

A man of the Ansar had passed away on that day. His name was Malik b. Amr of Banu al-Najjar clan. The Messenger of God led his janaza (funeral) prayer, and then came out to the people. The people were now remorseful and said, "We have forced the Messenger of God (to do something against his will), and we have no right to do so."

When the Messenger of God came out to them, they said, "O Messenger of God, we have pushed you to take this decision, and it is wrong of us. If you want, please stay, and may God's blessings be with you."

The Messenger of God said, "It is not fitting for a prophet to take off his armor after wearing it, until after the battle."
And the Messenger of God marched out in the company of a thousand of his companions.

A VALIANT WOMAN FIGHTS TO PROTECT THE PROPHET (PBUH) AT UHUD

Nusayba Bint Ka'ab, mother of 'Umara and wife of Ghazia b. 'Amr, participated in the battle of Uhud, along with her husband and son.
Ibn Hisham writes: "Umm 'Umara (Nusayba) Bint Ka'ab al-Mazinia fought at Uhud. Sa'id b. Abu Zaid al-Ansari states that Ummu Sa'ad Bint Sa'ad b. Rabi'a used to say, I went to see Umm 'Umara (Nusayba)' and told her, 'Please tell me your story.' So she said:

'I went out early in the morning to see how the people were doing. I had with me a jar of water. So I went up to the Messenger of God, who was with his companions. And the Muslims had the upper hand. When the Muslims were routed, I rushed alone to the Messenger of God. I started defending him with my sword and by shooting arrows with a bow until I received all my wounds.'

She (Ummu Sa'ad) went on to say: 'I saw a scar on her shoulder. It was deep. So I said, 'Who inflicted this on you?' She said, 'Ibn Qamia. May God curse him! When the people (some Muslim fighters) abandoned the Messenger of God, he approached saying, 'show me where Muhammad is. I have not won if he is alive.' So Mus'ab b. 'Umair and I obstructed him. And some people were among those who stood their ground with the Messenger of God. So he hit me as you see. I also hit him, but the enemy of God wore two armors.'"

BILAL IS IN TROUBLE

'Abdullah b. Lahiyi al-Howzani said, "I met Bilal–the Muadhin (the person who makes the call to prayer) of the Messenger of God, and said, 'Tell me about the Messenger of God's spending habits.'"

He said, "He used to possess nothing. Since God raised him as a prophet, he entrusted me with such issues until his death.

Whenever a needy Muslim person came to ask for help, he would have me take a loan in order to help the person with clothing and food.

One day, a polytheist approached me and said, 'Bilal, I have comfortable means. Do not, therefore, ask anyone except me for loans. Anytime you need some money, you can count on me, and don't have to go around looking for it elsewhere,' and I agreed. So I began to borrow from him. One day, after making my ablutions, when I was about to call out for prayer, the polytheist appeared along with a group of traders. When he saw me he said, 'You Abyssinian.' I said, 'Yes, here I am.' He began to say vile things. Then he said, 'Do you know how many days are left for the end of the month?' I said,

'Close.' He said, 'Exactly four days from now. Then, I will take you in return for the loans. I didn't grant you the loans out of good will for you or for your companion. I only did so that you can become my slave legally, and return to rearing cattle as before.'

The man's threat shook me profoundly. I left and made the prayer call. After I prayed the Isha (the fifth daily prayer) and the Prophet (pbuh) had retired to his home for the night, I knocked on his door and sought permission to see him. He invited me in.

I said, 'O Messenger of God, the polytheist I spoke to you about, from who I have been taking loans said such and such. You do not have anything with which to release me, nor do I have anything. And he is threatening to humiliate me. Please grant me the permission to escape and seek refuge with some unknown and newly converted Muslims, until God grants His Messenger what I need for my release (from the debt).' He said, 'Leave if you wish.' So I left. When I got home, I placed my sword, my quiver, my shield and my sandals by my head, and stared into the sky above.

Each time I tried to catch some sleep, I would wake up after an hour. If I saw that there was still some night left, I would sleep again. I did this until I saw the streaks of dawn. As I was about to continue my journey, I saw a man running toward me and calling me, 'Bilal, the Messenger of God wants you to return.' So I set out on my return until I got to him (Prophet [pbuh]).

I saw four tied camels with loads of goods. I came to the Messenger of God and asked for permission to come in. He (the Prophet [pbuh]) said to me, 'Rejoice for God has brought your ransom.' I thanked God, and he (the Prophet [pbuh]) said 'Did you come across the four tied camels? 'I said, 'Yes.' He said, "The camels and their load–clothes and food—are gifts to me from the ruler of Fadak. They are all yours. Take them and pay back your debt.'

I did. I offloaded them, secured them, and left to make the call for the morning prayer. After the Messenger of God had prayed, I left for Baqia (burial ground in Madinah), put my fingers in my ears and shouted out, 'Whoever has granted a loan to the Messenger of God, let him come.'

Thus I started selling and settling loans until there remained in my hands only two Uqtas or an Uqta and a half (weight measures). Then I left for the mosque, and the day's congregants had dispersed. The Messenger of God sat there alone in the mosque. I greeted him, and he said, 'How have things gone?' I said, 'God has settled all the debts of the Messenger of God, and no debt remains.' The Messenger of God said, 'Did any goods remain?' I said, 'Yes.' He said, 'Please, make sure that you give me respite from it.' After he did the night prayers, he called me and said, "How did things go?" I said, 'What remains is with me; no one came.'

He stayed in the mosque until dawn, and he remained in the mosque for a second day until late afternoon. Then two people came riding. I left with them, fed them, and clothed them. When he (the Prophet [pbuh]) finished his night prayers, he called me and said, 'How did things go?' I said, 'God has granted you respite from them, O Messenger of God.' He glorified God and thanked Him, moved by the fear he had of facing sudden death, while he had these (gifts and debts). Then I followed him until he came to his wives. He greeted each wife in turn, until he reached his dwelling for the day. This is the answer to your question."

CLOUDS, THEN SUNSHINE

Mundhir b. Jarir narrates a story his father told him: "We were with the Messenger of God early in the day when a group of people came to him. They hardly had clothes on; what they wore had patches of different colors. Their swords were hanging on their necks like necklaces. Most, in fact all of them were from Mudar. The face of the Messenger of God became pale at seeing such destitution. He went into his dwelling, came out and asked Bilal to make the call for prayer. After the prayer he started the sermon with the Qur'anic verses: *"O mankind fear your Lord who created you from a single soul. God is watching over you."* (4: 1). Give in charity a dinar, a dirham (currency), clothes, a measure of wheat, a measure of dates. Give even if it is half of a date.'

A man from the Ansar approached, carrying a bag that was so heavy he could carry it no more. Other people followed suit until I saw two big heaps of foodstuff and clothes. The Messenger's face glowed as if it were gold. Then he said, 'Whoever initiates a good Sunna (practice) in Islam will get its reward and then also the reward of those who act on it in the future, without there being any reduction in reward of those who act on that Sunna. And whoever initiates a bad practice in Islam will bare the weight of its evil reward, and also that of those who act on it in the future, without there being any reduction in the weight that the latter shall bear.'"

ABDULLAH B. 'UBAYY, THE BITTER ENEMY OF THE PROPHET AND MADINAH'S CHIEF HYPOCRITE DIES

'Abdullah b. 'Umar said: "When 'Abdullah b. 'Ubayy died, his son ('Abdullah, who was a Muslim) came to the Messenger of God and pleaded, 'O, Messenger of God give me your shirt, so that I can use it as a shroud for him. And please lead his funeral prayer, and ask God to forgive him.' The Messenger of God gave him his shirt and said, 'When you are done preparing him, call us.'

When 'Abdullah finished preparing his father, he called upon the Prophet, who came to lead the prayer. At that moment, 'Umar b. al-Khattab drew back the Prophet (by his cloak) saying, 'O Messenger of God, are you going to pray for him when God has enjoined you not to pray for the Munafiqin (hypocrites)?' The Prophet replied, 'I have a choice in the matter.' Quoting a verse from the Qur'an, he said, *"It matters not if you pray for their forgiveness or do not pray for it. (But) even if you pray for their forgiveness seventy times, God will not forgive them."* (9: 80).

The Prophet (pbuh) led the prayer. Later this verse was revealed: *"Never again pray for a confirmed hypocrite when he dies, and never stand at his grave"* (9: 84). He stopped praying for them (the hypocrites) from that day on.

A DIFFICULT MOMENT WITH A BELOVED SON

Anas b. Malik relates: "We went with the Messenger of God to Abu Saif al-Qain's house, who was the nurse of Ibrahim (the Prophet's son).

The Messenger of God took Ibrahim, kissed him and sniffed him. On another occasion, we went to see him (Ibrahim) and he was dying. The eyes of the Messenger of God started flowing with tears. Then Abd al-Rahman b. 'Auf, said, 'Even you, O Messenger of God (weep)?'

The Prophet said, 'O Ibn 'Auf, these are tears of mercy.'

Then again his tears fell, and he added, 'The eyes are in tears and the heart is afflicted, but we say nothing that displeases our Lord. O Ibrahim, we grieve at being separated from you.'"

A DATE PREVENTS HIM FROM SLEEPING

Amr b. Shuaib on the authority of his father and grandfather reported that the Prophet found a date under his side at night and ate it. He could not sleep that night afterwards. Some of his wives said, "O Messenger of God, you did not sleep last night!" He said, "I found a date by the side (of my sleeping mat), and I ate it. And I had some charity dates with me; I feared that what I had eaten was one of them."

'A'ISHA REMEMBERS

Ata relates: "'Ubayyd b. Umair, 'Abdullah b 'Umar and I went to see 'A'isha (at her home). Ibn 'Umar said (to 'A'isha), 'Tell me the most amazing thing you saw in the messenger of God.' 'A'isha wept and then said, 'Everything about him was amazing. One night, he said, 'O 'A'isha, would you permit me to rise (from bed) to worship my Lord?' I said, 'But I love your breath and the closeness of your body to mine.' He got up and stood over the water skin in the house. He used very little water (in his ablutions). Then he stood up and started reciting the Qur'an. Then he wept until I saw that the tears had soaked his shirt collar. Then he leaned on his right side and placed his right hand on his cheek. He wept until I saw that the ground was soaked in his tears.

Then Bilal came to make the call to prayer. He saw him (the Prophet) weeping. Bilal said, 'O Messenger of God, are you weeping while God has forgiven your sins, those of the past and those of the future?' He replied, 'Should I then not be a grateful servant?' Then, he continued by saying, 'And how can I help crying when God revealed to me during the night the verse: *"Surely in the creation of the heavens and the earth, and the alternation of night and day are signs for the thoughtful."* (3: 190).

He then added, 'Woe to whoever reads this verse, and does not ponder on it.'"

WHAT HUNGER CAN DO

Abu Huraira said, "The Messenger of God, may God bless him and grant him peace, went out one day or night and came across Abu Bakr and 'Umar. He asked, 'What has brought both of you out of your houses at this time?' They said, 'Hunger, O Messenger of God.' He said, 'Me too. And by the One in whose hand is my soul, what brought you out has brought me out, so get up.'

They got up with him and went to the house of a man of the Ansar, but he was not home. But when his wife saw the Prophet (pbuh) she said, 'Welcome! Welcome!' The Messenger of God asked her, 'Where is so-and-so?' She replied, 'He went to fetch water.' When the Ansar man returned, he saw the Messenger of God and his two companions.' He said, 'Praise and thanks be to God. No one has more honorable guests today than I (have).'

He went and brought them a branch with unripe and ripe fresh dates on it and said, 'Eat.' He took a knife and the Messenger of God, may God bless him and grant him peace, said to him, 'Don't slaughter one which gives milk.' So he slaughtered for them and they ate from the sheep and from that branch and drank.

When they had eaten to their satisfaction and quenched their thirst, the Messenger of God, may God bless him and grant him peace, said to Abu Bakr and 'Umar, 'By the One who has my soul in His hand, you will be asked about this blessing on the Day of Resurrection. Hunger brought you out of your houses and you did not return until this blessing was bestowed upon you.'"

PREOCCUPATIONS AT HOME

Al-Aswad b. Yazid said, "'A'isha was asked, 'What did the Prophet, may God bless him and grant him peace, used to do in his house?' She said, 'He worked for his family. That means he was at their service. When the time for prayer came, he would then head for the prayers.'"

THE PROPHET AND THE TROUBLESOME BEDOUIN

Abu Huraira reports: "A Bedouin came to the Prophet and said, 'Give me something, Muhammad, because you are not giving from your own wealth, nor from the wealth of your father.' He became rough with the Prophet, and the Prophet's companions jumped forward and said, 'You enemy of God, how dare you speak like that to the Messenger of God?'

The Prophet said, 'I order you strictly to leave him alone,' and he invited him (the Bedouin) into his house, and gave him something, and said, 'Are you satisfied?' The Bedouin said, 'No.' Then he gave him more and said, 'Are you satisfied?' The Bedouin said, 'No.' He gave him for the third time, and said, 'Are you satisfied?' The Bedouin said, 'Yes.' The Prophet said, "Please return to my companions and inform them that you are now satisfied, for they now harbor something against you in their hearts.' Then the Prophet said to his companions, 'Do you know the similitude of this man and myself? It is like a man in the middle of the desert with his travel provisions and his riding camel. His animal ran away, and the people started chasing him. This only spurred the animal on in its escape. He (the man) said: 'Leave me alone with my camel, because I know her better than you.'

He lifted some grass from the ground and said to the animal: 'Ha, ha.' She returned and sat near his feet. He harnessed her, lifted the provisions and put them on her back, and rode her. If I had not restrained you after he said what he said, and you killed him and he would have entered hell.'"

EXCEPTIONALLY, THE PROPHET IS DISPLEASED WITH ABU BAKR

Abu Huraira relates that a man insulted Abu Bakr while he was in the company of the Prophet. The Prophet was amazed and smiled. The man continued his insults and Abu Bakr reciprocated some of the insults. At that point the Prophet became upset and got up and left. Abu Bakr caught up with him and said, "While he was insulting me you kept sitting, and when I reciprocated some of the insults, you became upset and left!" The Prophet said, 'There was an angel by you speaking in your defense, and when you reciprocated some of the insults, Satan (came and) sat, and I do not sit with Satan."

Then he added, "O Abu Bakr, there are three statements, all of which are true: No servant of God is unjustly treated and yet restrains himself for Almighty God's sake, except that God increases His support of him. No one opens the gate of giving to promote good human ties for God's sake, except that God increases him in sufficiency. And no one opens the door of begging seeking thereby wealth, except that God, the Magnificent, increases his insufficiency."

HAPPY AT LAST

Abu Huraira narrates: "A Bedouin came to the Prophet and asked, 'Who will be the Judge of Creation at Resurrection, O Messenger of God?' The Messenger answered, 'God.' The Bedouin said, 'By the Lord of the Ka'aba, we are saved!' The Prophet (pbuh) said, 'How come, O Bedouin?' He replied, 'One who is generous will always forgive once he has the upper hand.'"

Makhul narrates: "A very old man came (to the Prophet [pbuh]). His eyebrows had grown over his eyes. He said, 'O Messenger of God, hear the case of a man who is treacherous and sinful, who indulges in all that his base soul tempts him with. If his sins were to be divided among the people of the earth, they would perish.' Then the Prophet asked, 'Would you embrace Islam?' He replied, 'As for me, I testify that there is no deity except God, alone without partners, and that Muhammad, the son of 'Abdullah, is His Servant and Messenger.' The Prophet then said, 'As long as you remain faithful to this, God will forgive all your sins, and he will transform your wrongdoings into good works.' The old man said, 'O Messenger of God, and my treachery, and my debauchery?' The Prophet replied, 'And your treachery, and your debauchery.'

The man then turned around to leave chanting, 'God is Great! There is no deity other than God.'"

WOMAN'S INTIMATE QUESTION

Ummu Salama said: "Umm Sullaim came to the Messenger of God and said, 'O Messenger of God, God does not shy away from the truth. Should a woman take a bath (ghusl) after a wet dream?' The Prophet (pbuh) said, 'If she sees the semen.' Umm Salama covered her face, and said, 'O Messenger of God, do women wet dream?' He said, 'It is alright (Umm Salama). Yes, how else does a child come to resemble his mother?'"

ABLE BUT FALSE ADVOCACY

Umm Salama (the prophet's wife) said: "Two men of the Ansar brought their dispute to the Messenger of God regarding an inheritance, whose document had been erased, and for which there was no clear evidence. The Messenger of God said, 'You are making your arguments to me, while I am only a man. Perhaps one of you is more articulate in making his case than the other. And I will make my verdict based on what I hear. So whomever I rule in favor of, while he is in fact wrong, let him not take his brother's right. For indeed, I would have simply sliced for him a great block of hellfire, which will be wrapped around his neck in the Day of Judgment.'

The two men wept, and each one of them said, 'I grant my right to my brother.' The Messenger of God then said, 'Based on what you have said, go back. Try to find the truth of the matter, and divide the property accordingly. Then let each one of you absolve the other of any mistake that might have been done in the dividing.'"

RESCUING A SLAVE

Abu Mas'ood al-Badri said: "I was flogging a slave of mine with a whip, when I heard a voice behind me, 'Be aware, O Abu Mas'ood!' I did not understand what was being said, because I was in such anger. But when he (the person calling) got closer to me, behold it was the Messenger of God. He said, 'Beware, Abu Mas'ood.'

I dropped the whip. He said, 'Know Abu Mas'ood, that God has more power over you than you have over this slave.' I said, 'Never again will I flog a slave.'"

In another narration: "I said, 'O Messenger of God, In God's name I free him.' He (pbuh) said, 'If you had not done that, the fire (of hell) would have scorched you.'"

A LIGHT MOMENT WITH AN OLD LADY

Al-Hassan said: "An old lady came to the Messenger of God and said, 'O Messenger of God, please pray for me so that I will be admitted into paradise.' He said, 'O Mother of so and so, old women can not enter paradise.' She turned around, and started crying. He said, 'Please tell her that when she enters it, she will not be old. For God had said, "*Verily, We have created them (maidens) of special creation. And made them virgins. Loving (their husbands only), (and) of equal age.*"' (56: 35-37)

PERHAPS IT WILL BE MY BURIAL SHROUD

Sahal b. Sa'ad said: "A woman came to the Prophet with a brand new burda, and he (Sahal) said to the assembly, 'Do you know what a burda is?' The people said, 'It is a cloak.' He said, 'Yes.' She (the woman) said, 'I knitted it with my hands. I came to dress you up with it.' The Prophet took it, as he was badly in need of it, and wore it. He then came out to us clad in it. A man thought that it was very beautiful, and said, 'Please clothe me with it. It is so beautiful!'

The people (present) said, 'That was not right. You saw how much the Prophet was in need of it, and then you asked him for it. You know very well that he is never asked for anything and he refuses to give it.' He said, 'By God, I did not request it to wear it. I only requested it, so that it will be my burial shroud.' Sahl said, 'It was indeed his burial shroud.'"

THE STUMP OF A DATE PALM WEEPS

Jabir b. 'Abdullah narrates: "The Prophet used a date palm stump as a pulpit for his Jumu'a (Friday) Khutba (sermon on sixth-day). One day, a woman or man of the Ansar said, 'O Messenger of God, shall we not make you a pulpit?' He replied, 'Yes, if you wish.' So they made him a pulpit. At the time of the Jumu'a prayers, the Prophet was led to the new pulpit. And the date palm uttered a sound similar to that of a weeping child. The Prophet came down (the pulpit) and hugged the date palm just as one would hug a crying child to calm him. He said, 'She (the stump) was crying, because she misses the joy of hearing the Dhikr (Remembrance of God) being conveyed close to her.'"

43

"I Feared That I Will Not See You."

'A'isha relates: "A man came to the Prophet and said, 'O Messenger of God, you are more beloved to me than myself, and you are dearer to me than my son. When I am at home, and think of you, I can find no peace until I rush to come and see you. But when I think of my death and your death, I realize that when you enter Paradise, you will be raised in rank along with the other Prophets. And I fear that if I enter Paradise, I will not see you.'

The Prophet did not say anything to him until the Angel Gabriel came down with the following verse:

Whoever obeys God and the Prophet, behold, they will be in the company of those that God has granted His favor: the Prophets, the truthful ones, the martyrs and the righteous. What a beautiful fellowship indeed!'" (4: 69)

Water and Dates

'A'isha narrates that she said to Urwa, "O Nephew, we used to watch the new moon: one moon, then the next, then the third. It would be two months, and all the while no cooking fire had been lit in any of the houses of the Messenger of God." Urwa said, "O my Aunt, what then did you eat to survive?" 'A'isha said, "The Aswadan, that is dates and water, except that the Messenger of God used to have neighbors among the Ansar, who had an animal with milk, and would give the Messenger of God some of their milk, which he used to make us drink it."

"I Only Shunned Your Name," Says 'A'isha

'A'isha said: "The Messenger of God said to me, 'I can always tell whether you are pleased with me or not.' I said, 'How do you know?' He said, 'When you are happy with me, you would say, 'by the Lord of Muhammad.' And when you are upset with me, you would say, 'by the Lord of Abraham (Ibrahim).'' I said, 'How true! But, by God, I shunned only your name.'"

TROUBLE IN THE HOUSEHOLD

Ibn Abbass said: "I was still eager to ask 'Umar about the two women, among the wives of the Prophet, alluded to by God in the verse:

'If (the two of) you repented to God (it will be better for you), though your hearts are so inclined (to opposing what the prophet likes).'

Then 'Umar made the pilgrimage, and I did the same, in his company. While on the road, he went off the road with a water jar, and I followed him. He relieved himself and came to me. I poured water in his hands, and he made the ablutions. I said to him, 'O Commander of the Faithful, who are the two women, among the wives of the Prophet, alluded to by God in the verse 'If you repented to God...'?'

'Umar replied, 'What a strange question, O Ibn Abbass! They are Hafsa and 'A'isha. We, the people of Quraish, always had the upper hand with our wives. When we came to Madinah, we found a people whose wives had the upper hand. Then our wives started learning from their wives. My house was in the quarter of Banu Ummaya b. Zaid in the outskirts of Madinah. One day I was upset with my wife, and behold she was arguing with me, and I could not stand her arguing with me. So she said, 'You are upset that I am arguing with you. But by God, the wives of the Prophet argue with him (the Prophet). And one of them would even shun him for an entire day.' So I left the house and headed for Hafsa's household. I went in and asked, 'Do you argue with the Messenger of God?' She said, 'Yes.' I said, 'Would one of you shun him all day?' She said, 'Yes.' I said, 'Whoever among you does that is certainly doomed! Aren't you afraid of God's wrath caused by His Prophet's anger? Certainly she is doomed! Don't you ever dare argue with the Messenger of God, and don't ask him anything! Ask me what you want. And do not be jealous that your neighbor ('Aisha) is more beautiful and more beloved to the Messenger of God than you.'

And I had a neighbor among the Ansar, and we used to alternate our visits to the Messenger of God. I would visit on one day, and he would on another and bring me news of any (new) revelation and other matters, and I did the same. And we spoke about the people of Ghassan, who were readying their horses in order to attack us. My friend visited (the Prophet) and came to me in the evening. He knocked on my door and called out to me. I came out to meet him. He said, 'Something momentous happened!' I said, 'What is it? Has Ghassan arrived?' He said, 'No, more momentous than that and of greater consequence. The Prophet has divorced his wives.' I said, 'Hasfa is doomed forever!' I thought this would happen one day. So after I did my morning prayers, I wore my clothes tightly around me, and left (for Hafsa's house). I went in and found her crying. I said to her, 'Did the messenger of God divorce (all of) you?' She replied, 'I don't know. He has distanced himself from us. He is over there by the watering spot.

I came to a Black servant of his and said, 'Please ask for me if I can come in.' He went in then came out and said, 'I mentioned you, but he did not say anything.'

So I left and came to the pulpit (of the mosque). I sat, and behold there was a group sitting around it (the pulpit). And some of them were weeping. I sat for a short while, and what was going on overwhelmed me. I went (back) to the servant and told him, 'Please, seek permission for 'Umar (to enter).' He went in, then came out and said, 'I mentioned you, but he did not say anything.'

So I turned my back to leave, and suddenly the servant called me back, and said, 'Go inside; he has given his permission.' I entered and greeted the Messenger of God, who was leaning on a mat that had left its marks on his side. I asked, 'Have you divorced your wives, O Messenger of God?'

He raised his head to me and said, 'No.' I said, Allahu Akbar (God is the greatest)! You know, O Messenger of God, that we Quraish, used to have the upper hand over our wives, but when we came to Madinah, we found a people whose wives had the upper hand. Then our wives started learning from their wives.

One day I was upset with my wife, and behold she was arguing with me, and I could not stand her arguing with me. So she said, 'You are upset that I am arguing with you. But by God, the wives of the Prophet argue with him (the Prophet). And one of them would even shun him for an entire day.' I said, 'Whoever among you does that is certainly doomed! Aren't you afraid of God's wrath caused by His Prophet's anger? Certainly she is doomed!"

The Messenger of God smiled.

And I said, "I had gone to Hafsa and had told her, 'Do not argue with the Messenger of God, and do not ask him anything. Ask me what you want. And Do not be jealous that your neighbor ('Aisha) is more beautiful and more beloved to the Messenger of God than you."

He smiled again.

I said, 'May I enjoy your company for a while, O Messenger of God?'

He said, 'Yes.'

So I sat down, and I lifted my eyes toward the ceiling, and I saw nothing remarkable except three skin jars. I said, 'Messenger of God, please pray that God grant a comfortable life to your people, for God has given affluence to Persia and Rome, and they do not worship him.'

He sat up straight and said, 'Are you in any doubt, Ibn al-Khattab? They are a people whose enjoyment has been hastened for them in the life of this world.'

I said, 'O Messenger of God, please ask for my forgiveness.'

He had sworn not to enter their houses for a month, because of the extreme frustration they caused him until God, the Majestic, rebuked him.'"

THE PROPHET'S (PBUH) BED

'A'isha said: "A woman of the Ansar visited me, and she saw the sleeping mat of the Prophet (pbuh), a rolled piece of cloth. So she sent me a sleeping mat made of wool. The Prophet then visited me and asked, 'What is this, 'A'isha?' I said, 'O Messenger of God, an Ansar woman visited me and saw your sleeping mat. She left and sent me this.'

He said, 'Return it, 'A'isha. By God, if I wished, God would provide for me a mountain of gold and silver.'"

A TRAVELER'S SLEEPING QUARTERS

'Abdullah b. Mas'ood said: "I visited the Prophet (pbuh) and he was in one of his rooms. It looked like a pigeon's house. He was sleeping on a straw mat, which had left marks on his skin. I wept.

He said, 'Why are you crying, O 'Abdullah?'

I said, 'O Messenger of God, Khosrow and Kaiser walk on luxurious silk, while you are sleeping on a straw mat that has left marks on your skin.' He said, 'Don't cry, 'Abdullah. This world is theirs, and the Hereafter is for us. I am like a traveler on his mount.' He came under a tree (briefly) and then departed."

'A'ISHA RACES WITH HER HUSBAND

'A'isha said: "The Messenger of God challenged me to a running race, and I outran him. After a while, I put on some weight, and he challenged me to a race. He won and said, 'This one for that one.'"

DEFENDING MADINAH AGAINST A GREAT COALITION OF ENEMY TRIBES

Jabir b. 'Abdullah says: "We were digging the trench along with the Messenger of God. Then I took leave of the Messenger and went home. I had a young she-goat at home. She was fat and strong.

I said to my wife, 'What if we prepared this for the Messenger of God?'

I asked my wife to prepare something, and she grinded some wheat, made some bread, and slaughtered the sheep, which we roasted for the Messenger of God. In the evening, as the Messenger of God was about to leave—we used to work in it (the trench) during the day and return to our families in the evening—I said, 'O Messenger of God, we had a small she-goat which we have prepared for you, along with some bread of barley. I would like you to come home with me.' I wanted him to come alone. He said, "Fine," and asked someone to shout aloud, "Come with the Prophet to the house of Jabir!"

I said, 'We belong to God, and to Him we shall return (this is usually uttered by someone struck by a calamity).' The Messenger came, and with him the multitudes. He sat down and we brought out the meal. He uttered his blessings, uttered the name of God, and ate. And the people kept coming to the food in turns. As soon as one group of people finished eating to their satisfaction, they got up and another group came until all the people of the trench came and left (after eating to their satisfaction)."

ANOTHER VERSION OF THE STORY

Abd al-Wahid b. Ayman went to Jabir, and his father said: "On the day of the trench, we came across a huge boulder, and we came to the Prophet and said, 'We have found that boulder in the trench.' He said, 'I will go down.' He stood up, and tied around his stomach was a stone (a way of reducing the pangs of hunger). And we had been working for three days without tasting a morsel of food. The Prophet took the pickaxe and struck the boulder, which was reduced to dust.

I said to the Prophet, 'Please give me leave to go home.'

I said to my wife, 'I saw something with the Prophet that I could not bear to see. Do you have anything?'

She said, 'I have some barley and a small goat.' She slaughtered the goat and she grinded the barley. Then we put the meat in the pot to cook.

When the flour had kneaded and the food was nearly cooked, I went to the Prophet. I said, 'I have a little food for you, you and one other person, or two persons.' He said, 'How much is the food?' I told him, and he said, 'It is good and sufficient.' He said, 'Tell her not to take off the pot or remove the bread from the oven until I arrive.' The prophet said to the people, 'Come on, let us go.' The immigrants and the helpers all got up. When I came to my wife, I said, 'Woe to you, the Prophet has come with the immigrants and the helpers, and whoever else is with them.' She said, 'Did he ask you (about the quantity of the food)?' 'Yes,' I said. The Prophet said, 'Come in, do not push or shove.'

He started breaking up the bread and spreading the meat over the pieces of bread. Meanwhile, he kept the pot simmering and covered it as well as the oven. He would take some bread from it, until everyone had his fill, and there was food left. Then he said to my wife, 'Eat this and give away some, for the people have been afflicted by extreme hunger.'

DIRE CIRCUMSTANCES DURING THE DEFENSE OF MADINAH

Hudhiafa said: "By God, you saw us with the Messenger of God at the trench. The Messenger of God prayed a portion of the night. He then turned to us and said, 'Who among you men is willing to go and find out what the folks (the enemy troops) have done and come back? I shall pray to God for him (the volunteer) to be my close companion in Paradise.'

No one stood up; so intense was the fear, the hunger and the cold. As no one stood up the Messenger of God called me, and I had no choice but to stand up when he called me. He said, 'O Hudhayfa, stand and go penetrate the ranks of the folks. See what they are up to. Make sure you do not initiate anything until you return to me.'

So I went and got into the midst of the folks. The winds and God's other forces were wreaking havoc. No pot or pan stood upright, no fire could be maintained, no structure was stable. Abu Sufyan stood up and said, 'People of Quraish, let everyone make sure of the person sitting next to him.'

I took the hand of the man next to me and asked him, 'Who are you?' He said, 'I am so and so, the son of so and so.'

Abu Sufyan then said, 'People of Quraish, you have not woken up at a place where one can stay. Our horses and camels have been decimated, and the Jews of Qurayzah have not fulfilled their promises to us. We hate the news coming to us about them. We have faced the cruel intensity of the wind as you can see. No pot of ours is still, no fire will light for us, and no tent is stable. Depart, therefore, for I am departing.'

He then stood by his tied camel. He sat upon it and hit it. It sprang up with him on three legs. By God he did not release the camel's fetter until he had stood up. If it were not for my pledge to the Messenger of God that I would initiate nothing until I returned to him, I could have killed him with an arrow had I wanted.

I came back to the Messenger of God, and he was standing in prayer, clad in a garment belonging to one of his wives. It had the picture of a saddle.

When he saw me, he drew me to himself and placed me between his legs, and covered me with a portion of the garment. He went to make his bowing and prostration, while I was under him. When he concluded his prayer with the invocation of peace I gave him my report."

CHICKS SEPARATED FROM THEIR MOTHER

'Amir al-Rami, the brother of Khudr, said: "I was in my country when I saw a raised flag. So I asked, 'What is that?' They said, 'It is the flag of the Messenger of God (pbuh).' So I came to him (the Prophet [pbuh]). He was under a tree, where a piece of cloth had been spread for him. He was sitting on it. His companions were gathered around him, and I sat in their midst. Then the Messenger of God spoke about diseases. He said, 'When the believer is afflicted with an illness and he recovers, that serves as expiation for the sins he committed in the past, and an admonition for the future. But when a hypocrite falls ill and recovers, he is like the camel. Its owner tied it up and then released it. But it has no clue why they tied it and why they released it. A man in the group said, 'O Messenger of God, what is illness? By God, I have never fallen ill." The Messenger of God said, 'Get up and leave. You are not one of us.'

As we were still there with the Prophet, a man approached. He carried something in his hand wrapped up in a piece of cloth. He said, 'O Messenger of God, I decided to come to you when I saw you. I passed through a wood, and heard the voices of young birds, and I took and put them in my cloth. Then their mother came fluttering around my head. I uncovered the young and the mother fell down upon them, then I wrapped them up in my carpet, along with their mother. Here they are with me.'

The Messenger of God said, 'Release them.' The man released them, but their mother refused to be parted from them. The Messenger of God said to his companions, 'Do you wonder at the affection of the mother towards her young?' They said, 'Yes, O Messenger of God'

He said, 'I swear by Him, who has sent me with the truth, God is more merciful to His creatures than the mother to her chicks. Return them, along with their mother, to the place from which you took them and release them. He returned them."

AT THE MARKET: WHAT IS THIS, O FOOD VENDOR?

Abu Huraira relates that the Messenger of God once passed by a mound of food (at the market). He dug into the food with his hand, and his fingers became wet with water. He then said, "Food seller, what is this?" The man replied, "O Messenger of God, this is due to rain." The Prophet said, "Why didn't you put it (the soggy food) on top so that people can see it?" Then he added, "Any person who cheats is not one of us."

THE PROPHET MISSES A BLACK WOMAN OR MAN

Abu Huraira also reported that a black woman or black young man used to sweep the mosque. The Messenger of God, may God bless him and grant him peace, missed her and asked after her or him. They said, "She died." He said, "Why did you not inform me?" It was as if they thought little of her or him. He said, "Show me the grave." They directed him to it and he prayed over it. Then he said, "These graves are filled with darkness surrounding their inhabitants. God Almighty illuminates them for them, by my praying over them."

JUDGING BETWEEN A JEW AND A MUSLIM

Abu Huraira narrates: "Once while a Jew was selling his goods, he was offered a price that he disliked. He said: "No, by Him who chose Moses over all human beings!"

An Ansar man, who had heard him, slapped him on the face and said: "You say, 'By Him who chose Moses over all human beings,' while we have the Messenger of God in our midst.'

The Jew went to the Prophet (pbuh) and said: 'O Abu-l-Qasim (Muhammad)! I am under the assurance and contract of security. And here a man slapped me.' The Prophet asked (the other man): 'Why have you slapped this man?" He said: 'O Messenger of God, he had said: 'by Him who chose Moses over all human beings while we have you in our midst.' The Prophet became so angry that his anger could be seen on his face. He said: 'Don't ascribe discriminatory ranks to God's prophets. When the trumpet will be blown everyone on the earth and in the heavens will swoon except those whom God will exempt.

Then the trumpet will be blown a second time and I will be the first to be resurrected, or at the head of those who are first resurrected. And behold I shall see Moses holding God's Throne! I will not know whether he swooned as he had done in Thur, or that he rose from the dead before I did! I cannot (even) say that any Prophet is better than Jonah Ibn Matah (who was swallowed by a whale).

TEACHING MODERATION IN RELIGIOSITY

Abdullah Ibn 'Umar Ibn Al-As narrates: "I used to fast everyday and read the Qur'an every night. Someone mentioned that to the Messenger of God, who sent for me. When I arrived he said: "Is what I have been told true, that you fast every day and read the Qur'an every night?" I said: "Yes, O Prophet of God, but I only intend good by so doing." He said: "It is sufficient that you fast for three days in every month." I said: "O Prophet of God, but I can do more than that." He said: "But your wife has rights over you; your body has rights over you; and your visitors have rights over you. And your body has rights over you."

THE ANSAR DISAGREE WITH THE PROPHET (PBUH) ON THE ISSUE OF GHATFAN

The Messenger of God sent a delegation to Uyinah b. Hisn b. Hudhaifa, b. Badr and to al-Harith, b. 'Auf, b. Abu Haritha al-Murri, who were both chieftains of the Ghatfan tribe. He offered them a third of the dates of Madinah if they and their people reconciled with the Prophet and his companions and agreed to a peace treaty. The treaty had not yet been made binding through witnesses. It just expressed a good intention. Before the Messenger of God could make the treaty official, he summoned Sa'ad b. Muadh and Sadd b. Ubada, informed them about his intention, and sought their advice.

54

They said to him, "O Messenger of God, is it an action that we do because we love it, or something that is ordered by God which we have to do, or is it something that you yourself have come up with for us?" He said, "Something I came up with. And by God, I am not doing this except because of the fact that the Arab tribes have united against you. I therefore wanted to break the noose around you to some extent."

Sa'ad b. Muadh said to him, "O Messenger of God, Ghatfan and we were polytheists and worshipped idols. We neither worshipped God, nor knew him. At that time they got none of the dates of Madinah except as our guests or through trade. Now that God has honored us (with Islam), guided us, and dignified us through you and through it, should we then give them our wealth? No, by God, we shall not give them anything but the sword until God decides between us and them."

"As you please," replied the Prophet (pbuh). Sa'ad b. Muadh took the document, erased what was written on it, and said, "Let them fight us. Let them persist in opposing us."

'A'ISHA, THE PROPHET'S (PBUH) BELOVED WIFE, IS ACCUSED

'A'isha relates: "It was the habit of the Messenger of God whenever he was about to travel to make a toss among his wives. The wife, whose arrow won, would accompany the Prophet (pbuh).

At the time of one his expeditions, the toss favored me and I traveled with him. This was after the verse on the hijab (the head covering for women) had been revealed.

I mounted my howdaj (a comfortable tent mounted on a camel), and was housed in it during the journey.

When the expedition was over, the caravan set out on its return trip to Madinah. We camped on a spot close to Madinah. At night, the Messenger of God gave his permission for the journey to start. When the permission was announced, I stood up and walked until I was able to leave the army behind, in order to find a place to relieve myself. After I relieved myself, I started walking back to my mount. At that point I passed my hand over my chest, and behold my necklace had fallen off.

I returned to the spot (where I had relieved myself) and started looking for it, until the search for it overwhelmed me. Meanwhile the people, who were in control of my camel, came to my camel and mounted my haudaj, believing that I was in it. At the time, women were very lanky; they had not yet put on weight. They used to eat very little. They (the tenders of my mount) were not alerted by the weight of the haudaj, as they prepared it, mounted it and led the camel away.

I was a very young girl at the time. They mounted the camels and set off on their journey. I finally found my necklace. Meanwhile the army had left. I came to the spot where we had encamped and found no one.

I decided to stay on the spot where I was, hoping that the people would realize that I was not with them and would come back to get me. As I sat on my spot, sleep overcame my eyes, and I slept.

Safwan b. al-Muattal of the tribe of Sulaym was traveling behind the army. He saw the dark shadow of a sleeping human being, moved toward me, and recognized me when he saw me. And he had seen me previously unveiled before I started wearing the veil. I woke up just as he exclaimed 'To God we belong, and to Him we shall return' upon seeing me. I covered my face with my cloak. By God, he did not utter a word to me, and I did not hear a word from him other than "To God we belong, and to Him we shall return.' He dismounted from his camel, which lay down. Then I climbed on it, and he led the camel until we caught up with the army, which had arrived in the searing heat of the early afternoon.

Those who destroyed themselves on my account destroyed themselves, chief among them was 'Abdullah b. Ubayy b. Salul.

Shortly after our arrival in Madinah, I felt very ill for a month. The people were busy spreading the calumny about me, and I had no idea that was going on.

In my pain, I was troubled and perplexed, because I did not see in the Messenger of God the kindness and attention I got from him in the past whenever I was ill. He would simply come in (to my dwelling), greet and say, 'How is this one doing?'

This troubled me greatly, but I did not sense anything particularly wrong. One day, I went out, after I started feeling better. I came out with Umm Mistah to the place where we usually relieved ourselves. We women only came to this place at night. This was before Arabs started to have toilets close to our houses. Our usage was that of the first Arabs in the matter of relieving ourselves. It was very hard on us when we started having toilets close to our houses.

So, I went out with Umm Mistah, the daughter of Abu Ruhm b. al-Muttalib, b. Abdu Manaf. Her mother was the daughter of Sakhr b. Amir, the aunt of Abu Bakr al-Siddiq. Her son was Mistah b. Uthatha b. Abbad b. al-Muttalib. So we went out, Bint Ruhm, and I to the back of my house, where we relieved ourselves. Umm Mustah tripped on her dress and she said, 'Confound Mistah!' I said, 'Come on, how can you say such a thing? How could you insult a man who witnessed the battle of Badr?' She said, 'Haven't you heard what he said?' I said, 'What did he say?' She then spoke to me about the scandal that was being spread (concerning me). My illness became severe. When I returned to my house, the Messenger of God came into my dwelling, greeted and said, 'How is this one doing?'

I said, 'Please, let me return to my parents!' I wished at that point to find out the truth of the matter from them (my parents). The Messenger of God gave me leave. I went to my parents and said to my mother, 'O Mom, what are the people saying?' She said, 'O my daughter, do not be hard on yourself. By God, no woman is loved dearly by her husband, and she has co-wives, except that these would conspire against her.' I said, 'Glory be to God, are people speaking about this?' I wept that night, with the tears never stopping to flow, and with no sleep, morning came, and I was still crying.

The Messenger of God called Ali b. Abu Talib and Usama b. Zaid when the revelation stopped coming down for a period of time. He wanted to seek their opinion on the separation of his wife. As for Usama, he indicated to the Messenger of God what he knew as to the innocence of his family, as well as the love he felt within him toward them. He said, 'O Messenger of God, they are your household, and we know nothing but good regarding them.' As for Ali b. Abu Talib, he said, 'God has not put any constraints on you, and there are many women beside her. If you ask her maid, she would tell you the truth.'

The Prophet (pbuh) called Barira and asked her, 'Have you seen anything that gave you some doubts regarding 'A'isha?' Barira replied, 'By He Who sent you (God) with the Truth, I have never noticed any fault in her other than that, being so young, she would occasionally doze off and let a domestic animal eat the dough.'

The Messenger of God then stood on the minbar (pulpit). He sought help against 'Abdullah Ibn Ubayy Ibn Salul. He said while on the minbar, 'O Muslims, who will support me against a man who has done great harm to my household? By God, I know nothing but good regarding my family. And they have been mentioning a man about whom I know nothing except good. He has never entered my household except in my presence.'

Sad b. Muadh from the Ansar, stood up and said, 'I will spare you his trouble. If he belongs to Aws (our tribe), I will hit his neck. If on the other

58

hand he belongs to the tribe of our brothers the Khazraj, you have only to give us your command.'

Sa'ad b. Ubada, the leader of the Khazraj and a man with a good reputation, stood up. He allowed his tribal feelings to get the better of him and said to Sa'ad b. Muadh, 'By God, you have lied. You shall not kill him, and you are not able to.' Usayd b. Hudayr, a cousin of Sa'ad b. Muadh, said to Sad b. Ubada, 'By God, you have lied. We will surely kill him. You are no more than a hypocrite defending hypocrites.' People belonging to the two tribes were very angry and were about to fight. The Prophet (pbuh) was still on the pulpit and he succeeded in his struggle to cool them down.

I kept crying for the rest of the day and did not sleep for two other nights. I could not sleep. Both my parents felt that crying would finally kill me.

As both of them sat close to me, while I was crying, a woman of the Ansar (helpers) sought permission to see me. I let her come inside. She sat and started weeping. As this was going on, the Messenger of God entered, greeted us, and sat down. And he had not sat in my dwelling since the start of the scandal. It had been a month, and no revelation had come down on my account. The Messenger of God made the tashahud (Testimony of Faith) as he sat, then said, 'A'isha, people have been saying such and such about you. If you are innocent, God will make your innocence known. If however you have committed a sin, ask for God's forgiveness and repent to him. When God's servant confesses his mistake and repents, God forgives him.'

When the Messenger of God finished, my tears dried up completely. I turned to my father and said, 'Answer on my behalf.' He said, 'By God, I do not know what to say to God's Messenger.' I then said to my mother, 'Answer on my behalf.' She said, 'By God, I do not know what to say to God's Messenger.'

I said, 'I am a young girl, and I cannot read much of the Quran. By God, I know that you have all heard this story so many times that it has found a home in your hearts, and you have come to believe it. If I should now say to you that I am innocent—and God knows that I am innocent—you will not believe me.

I can find no words to describe my situation and yours except what the father of Joseph said: 'So (for me) patience is most fitting. And I will seek God's help against that which you describe.'

I then turned around and lay on my bed. I knew that I was innocent and God would make my innocence known. But, by God, I did not expect that a revelation to be recited would be sent down on my account. I was much too ordinary for God to speak about me on any issue. But I was hoping that the Messenger of God would see a vision in his sleep in which God would show my innocence.

But before the Messenger of God left us, and before anyone in his household went out, God, the Exalted, brought down revelation to His Prophet.

The usual burden of the Revelation gripped him and overwhelmed him. In a cold winter day, he was soon covered in sweat that looked like stringed pearls as a result of the heaviness of the words that were descending upon him.

Then the grip was loosened, and he smiled. The first words he muttered were, 'Rejoice, 'A'isha, for God has declared your innocence.' My mother said to me, 'Stand up for him (the Prophet [pbuh])!' I said, 'By God, I will not stand up for him, and I will thank no one except God, who has proclaimed my innocence.' God, The Exalted sent down: *Behold those who spread slander, are a group among you.' (And) ten (subsequent) verses in regard to my innocence."*

A DIFFICULT CASE OF BETRAYAL

Ali relates: "God's Messenger sent al-Zubair, al-Miqdad and myself, saying, 'Proceed until you reach Rawdah Khakh (a garden). You will find a lady riding a camel. She has a letter. Take it from her!'

So we set out on our galloping horses and rode until we reached the Rawdah. There indeed we found the lady. We said to her 'Take out the letter.' She said, 'I do not have a letter.' We then said, 'You will take out the letter, or else we will strip you.' So she took it out of her braid, and we brought the letter to the Messenger of God. The letter was from Hatib b. Abu Balta'ah, and it was addressed to some idol-worshippers of Makkah. He was informing them about some of the (secret) plans of the Messenger of God.

The Messenger of God said, 'O Hatib, what is this?'

He said, 'O Messenger of God, please, do not be hasty with me. I was a person attached to Quraish, but was not one of them. Some of the emigrants with you have family ties with the people of Makkah, which will protect their relatives and their property. Because I lacked that (family connection), I wanted to do them a favor that will cause them to protect my relatives. I did not do this out of disbelief or apostasy, or because I approve of disbelief after I have become a Muslim.'

The Messenger of God said, 'He has spoken the truth to you.' 'Umar said, 'O Messenger of God, permit me to cut off the head of this hypocrite!' The Prophet said, 'He participated in the battle of Badr.

What do you know? Perhaps God has looked with favor at those who participated in Badr and said, 'O the people of Badr, do as you please, for I have forgiven you.'"

ABU SUFYAN B. AL-HARITH SEEKS RECONCILIATION WITH THE PROPHET (PBUH)

Al-Abbass set out with his family and relatives before the opening of

Makkah. He had become Muslim and was migrating to Makkah. He met the Messenger of God at the village of Jafna --- some say a little farther than that. Among those who met the Prophet (pbuh)on the way were his cousins Abu Sufyan b. al-Harith and 'Abdullah b. Abu Ummaya at the village of Abwa. These two were the son of the Prophet's (pbuh) uncle and the son of his aunt respectively. He turned away from them, because of the excessive way they used to hurt and insult him.

Ummu Salma said to him (the Prophet [pbuh]), 'Do not let the son of your uncle and the son of your aunt be the most deprived of your mercy.' And Ali said to Abu Sufyan, 'Come to the Messenger of God, face him directly and say to him what the brothers of Joseph said to Joseph (they said, *"By God, God has preferred you over us. And we were surely wrong in our actions.")* (12: 91)

He does not want anyone to excel him in gracious speech. Abu Sufyan did (what Ali advised him) and the Messenger of God said to him, *"Let there be no blaming on you today. May God forgive you, for He is the Most Merciful of those who are merciful."* (12: 92)

Abu Sufyan immediately composed and recited verses in praise of the Prophet Muhammad. He became a good Muslim from that point on. And it is said that he never once raised his head toward the Messenger of God since he embraced Islam, out of shyness."

ABU SUFYAN B. HARB SEEKS RECONCILIATION WITH THE PROPHET

Ibn Abbass narrates that the Messenger of God undertook to travel to Makkah in the Year of the Opening (of Makkah). He left Madinah in the charge of Abu Ruhm Khulthum b. Hussain al-Ghifari. He set out on the tenth day of the month of Ramadhan. So the Messenger of God fasted, and the people fasted with him. When he reached al-Kadid, which was between 'Usfan and Amaj, he broke his fast. He then continued on until he reached Marr al-Dhaharan (a valley) in the company of ten thousand Muslims from the tribes of Muzina and Sulaim and in every tribe there were a considerable number and Islam. The journey brought together in the company of the Messenger of God the Muhajiroon (the emigrants) and the Ansar (the helpers). None of them stayed behind. The Messenger of God reached Marr al-Dhahran. Quraish had no knowledge of his journey and had no news about him. And they do not know what he will do. On that night, Abu Sufyan b. Harb, Hakim b. Hizam, and Budail b. Warqa went out spying and listening for any news (about the Muslims).

Abbass b. Abd al-Muttalib (Ibn Abbass' father) came to the Messenger of God as the latter was on his way to Makkah. Abu Sufyan b. al-Harith b. al-Muttalib and 'Abdullah b. Abu Umayya b. al-Amughira had also come across the Messenger of God on the road between Makkah and Madinah. They desired to meet with him. Umm Salama spoke to him the Prophet, her husband, on their behalf. She said, "God's Messenger, they are your own cousins and one of them is also your father-in-law." He replied, "I have no need of them. My cousin defamed me and my aunt's son and father-in-law was the one who said what you know in Makkah."

The two were informed of the Prophet's (pbuh) response. Abu Sufyan, who had one of his sons with him, said "If he does not receive me, I will take this son of mine by the hand and we will both wander through the land until we die of starvation and thirst."

When the Messenger of God was told about this, he softened his stance. And so the two were made to come to the Prophet and embraced Islam.

When the Messenger of God stopped at Marr al-Dhahran, Abbass said, "Quraish has perished. If the Messenger entered Makkah by force before they obtained his amnesty, God would destroy them forever." So I sat on the white mule of the Messenger of God, rode it until I reached Al-Arak, and said, "Perhaps, I will find some woodcutters, or milkman, or some of the folk who would return to Makkah and inform the Meccans about the whereabouts of the Messenger of God. Perhaps they would then come out to meet with him and seek amnesty before he enters Makkah forcibly."

He said, "I kept on riding in order to accomplish my mission, which was brought about when I heard Abu Sufyan and Budail b. Warqa thinking matters over. Abu Sufyan had said, 'I have never seen what I saw today before; just fires and no army.' Budail had said, 'By God, those are the fires of Khuzah. War had kindled them.' Abu Sufyan had said, 'By God, Khuzah is much too weak and small for these to be their fires and their army.' I recognized his voice and said, 'O Abu Hanzala!' He recognized my voice and said, 'O Abu al-Fadl!' I said, 'Yes!' He said, 'What is going on? I will sacrifice my mother and father for you!' I said, 'Confound you, Abu Sufyan! There, is the Messenger of God among his people. Quraish has perished!' He said, 'I will sacrifice for you my father and my mother! What is the way out?' I said, 'By God, if he has victory over you, he will strike your neck. Ride, therefore, with me, so that I can take you to the Messenger of God, and ask him to grant you amnesty.'

So he rode behind me, and his companion returned (to Makkah). So I set out with him. Each time we passed by any of the fires (camps) of the Muslims, they (Muslim fighters) would say: "Who is this?" As soon as they saw the mule of the Messenger of God they would say: "O the uncle of God's Messenger riding on the Messenger's mule." Then we passed by 'Umar b. al-Khattab, who said: 'Who is this?" He approached me, and when he saw Abu Sufyan on the saddle of the mule, said: "Abu Sufyan, enemy of God! Praise be to God who has overpowered you and brought you here without a treaty or agreement (for your protection).' Then he rushed to the Messenger of God in a state of fury.

The mule sped and overtook him, just as a slow animal would overtake a slow man. So, I dismounted the mule, and entered the Messenger's dwelling followed by 'Umar, who said: "O Messenger, this is Abu Sufyan! God has overpowered him, and brought him here, with neither treaty nor agreement (for his safety). Please give me leave to chop off his head." I said: "O Messenger of God, I have given him sanctuary." Then I sat close to the Messenger of God and touched his head, saying: "No one other than me should talk to him tonight." And when 'Umar insisted on speaking against him, I said: "Take it easy 'Umar, by God, had he been a man of the clan of Addi b. Kaab, you would not have said this. But you know that he is one of the men of the Abdu Manaf clan." He said: "Take it easy, Abbass! By God your Islam the day you accepted it was dearer to me than the Islam of Khattab (my father) if he joined Islam. One thing I surely know is that your joining Islam was dearer to the Messenger of God than the Islam of Khattab if he joined Islam."

The Messenger of God said: "Abbass, take him to your mount. When he wakes up in the morning bring him to me." When he woke in the morning, I took him to the Messenger of God. When the Messenger saw him, he said: "Confound you Abu Sufyan! Is it not time for you to realize that there is no deity other than God?"

He said: "I am ready to sacrifice my father and mother for you! You are truly forbearing, generous and kind! By God, had there been any deity alongside God, he would have been of some use to me by now. "

He (the Prophet) said: "Confound you, Abu Sufyan! Is it not time for you to know that I am the Messenger of God?"
He (Abu Sufyan) said: "How forbearing, generous, and kind you are! On this point, I still have some doubts."

I (Abbass) said: "Come on man, embrace Islam and testify that that there is no deity but God and that Mohammad is God's Messenger, or be ready to lose your head." He then made his declaration of faith in Islam. I said: "O

Messenger of God, Abu Sufyan loves honor. Give him something. "Yes," the Prophet (pbuh) said, "whoever enters Abu Sufyan's house (in Makkah) is safe! Whoever stays indoors and closes his door is safe! Whoever enters the mosque is safe!"

THE PROPHET (PBUH) CALMS DOWN A MAN OVERAWED AT SEEING HIM

Abu Mas'ood said: "A man (in Makkah) came to the Prophet (pbuh). The Prophet (pbuh) spoke to him. He started trembling. The Prophet said to him, "Be at ease! I am not a king. I am merely the son of a woman who used to eat dried meat.'"

SA'AD B. UBADA, THE OVER EXCITED FLAG BEARER OF THE PROPHET (PBUH), IS DISMISSED

Sa'ad, who was carrying the flag of the Messenger of God, passed by Abu Sufyan shouting, "Today is a day of conflict and war; there is no more sanctuary. Today, God has humbled Quraish." The Messenger of God approached, and when he got close, Abu Sufyan said, "Messenger of God, have you ordered the killing of your people? Sa'ad and those with him claimed (so), as he passed by us saying, 'Today is a day of conflict and war; there is no more sanctuary.' And I ask you for God's sake to look after your people, for you are the most generous man, the most merciful man, and the man that is most honoring of family ties." 'Abdul Rahman b. 'Auf and 'Uthman b. Affan said, "We do not trust that Sa'ad will not cause havoc."

The Messenger of God said, "Today is the day of mercy and forgiveness; God has honored Quraish today."

The Messenger of God then sent for Sa'ad to take the flag from him and to be given to Qais son Sa'ad. The Messenger of God realized that the flag was not taken away from Sa'ad if he gave it to his son.

Sa'ad refused to hand over the flag without evidence from the Prophet (pbuh) (proving that the order is from him). The Messenger then sent again someone along with his turban. Sa'ad recognized it (the turban) and gave the flag to Qais, his son.

WHO KEEPS THE KEY TO THE KA'ABA NOW?

The Messenger of God came down from the Ka'aba on the day of the Opening of Makkah. He had with him the key to the Ka'aba. He retired to the mosque and sat. He had taken the office of giving the water to the pilgrims from Abbass, and he had taken the key (of the Ka'aba) from 'Uthman. When he sat down, he said, Call Uthman for me. Uthman b. Talha was called for him.

One day, years back, he (the Prophet) was inviting 'Uthman, who then had the key to the Ka'aba, to Islam. He had said, "Maybe someday you will see that key in my hands, and I will then give it to whom I please." 'Uthman said, "Quraish would certainly have been destroyed and humiliated before that day should come." He replied, "No, rather Quraish would be strong and mighty on that day."

So when he called 'Uthman after he had taken the key from him, 'Uthman remembered the Prophet's words (of many years back). 'Uthman approached the Prophet and came to him with a happy face, and he did likewise. The Prophet said, "Take it, O children of the Abu Talha clan forever and ever. No one will take it from you except an oppressor. O 'Uthman, God has entrusted His house to you. Derive your sustenance (from this office) with righteousness."

'Uthman turned to leave, the Prophet called him back, and he returned. The Prophet said, "Has not what I told you come to pass?"

'Uthman recalled his words of years back in Makkah and said, "It has, and I testify that you are the Messenger of God." He gave him the key, and the Prophet lay on the ground wrapped in his garment. The Prophet then said, "Safeguard it!"

THE PROPHET (PBUH) ADDRESSES THE MECCANS (EXCERPTS)

The Prophet (pbuh) said, "O people of Quraish, God has abolished the haughtiness of the pre-Islamic period and the arrogance based on family lineage (today). Every man is an offspring of Adam, and Adam is from dust."

The Prophet (pbuh) then recited the following Qur'anic verses: *"O mankind! Behold, we have created you male and female, and have made you into nations and tribes, so that you may come to know each other. Behold, the most honorable of you, in the sight of God, is the most righteous and pious. Behold, God is knower, well aware."* (49: 13)

He then said, "O Quraish, what do you think I will do with you now?"

They said, "Good. You are a noble brother, son of a noble brother."

He (the Prophet [pbuh]) said, "Go your way, for you are free."

THOUGHTS OF ASSASSINATION

Fudala b. 'Umayr b. al-Mulawah had the intention to kill the Messenger of God, who was then moving around the Ka'aba in the year that Makkah was opened (taken). As Fudala got close to him, the Prophet (pbuh) said, "Is that Fudala?"

He answered, "Yes, O Messenger of God."

He said, "What have you been saying to yourself?"

Fudala answered, "Nothing, I was only remembering God."

The Prophet (pbuh) laughed and said, "Ask God for His forgiveness."

The Prophet (pbuh) then placed his hand on Fudala's chest and brought peace to it.

Fudala used to say later, "By God, when he lifted his hand off my chest, there was nothing created by God dearer to me than him."

Fudala also said, "I returned to my family. I came across a woman on my way. I used to love talking to her. She said, 'Come on (Fudala), let us have a talk.' I said 'No.'"

'UMAYR WANTS HIS OLD FRIEND, SAFWAN, TO RECONCILE WITH THE PROPHET (PBUH)

Safwan b. Umaya escaped from Makkah and headed for Jeddah, in order to board a boat that would take him to Yemen. His old friend and co-conspirator, 'Umayr b. Wahab said, "O Prophet of God, Safwan b. Umaya is the leader of his people. He has fled in fear of you, in order to throw himself in the sea. Please, grant him amnesty. May God bless you!" The Prophet (pbuh) said, "I grant him amnesty."

'Umayr said, "O Messenger of God, give me a proof of your amnesty." The Prophet (pbuh) gave him his turban, the one with which he had entered Makkah.

'Umayr took it and headed for Jeddah. He caught up with Safwan just as he was about to board the boat. He said, "Safwan, By God, do not destroy your life. This is a testimony of the Prophet's (pbuh) amnesty for you. I have brought it with me." Safwan said, "Confound you! Get away from me, and do not speak to me." 'Umayr said, "No more of that! For you I would give my mother and father as ransom! Truly he (the Prophet [pbuh]) is the best, the kindest, the most gracious and benevolent of all people. He is your cousin. His might is your might! His honor is your honor! His dominion is your dominion!"

Safwan said, "I fear for my life."

'Umayr said, "He is much too kind and clement for you to have such fears."

So 'Umayr brought Safwan back to Makkah. When brought face to face with the Prophet (pbuh), Safwan said, "'Umayr claims that you granted me amnesty. Did you?"

The Prophet (pbuh) said, "Yes, he spoke the truth." Safwan said, "Grant me then a period of two months to think my position over."

The Prophet (pbuh) said, "You have four months to think over your position."

HIND FACES THE PROPHET (PBUH) ALONG WITH OTHER NON-MUSLIM WOMEN OF MAKKAH (Excerpts)

As for Hind Bint Utbah, wife of Abu Sufyan, it is said of her that she gave her oath of allegiance to the Prophet (pbuh) on the day of the opening of Makkah. The Prophet was on the hill of Safa, and 'Umar was close to him at the highest point of the hill's slope. She and other women of Quraish approached the Prophet (pbuh) to make the oath of allegiance to Islam. 'Umar spoke to them on the Prophet's behalf.

When they were told not to associate partners with God, Hind said, "We know that had there been a god other than God, he would have been able to help us."

When he said, "And do not steal," Hind said, "Would a free woman steal? But you see, O Messenger of God, Abu Sufyan is a stingy man; it may be that I take some money from him, without his knowing in order to take care of his son." The Prophet (pbuh) said, "Take from it what you and your child need, reasonably." And he added, "Are you Hind?" She answered, "Yes indeed, forgive the past, may God forgive you."

Abu Sufyan, who was present, said, "Whatever you have taken in the past is yours."

Then the Prophet (pbuh) said, "And not to commit fornication or adultery." She said, "Messenger of God, would a free woman commit fornication or adultery?"

Then he said (quoting the Qur'an), "They (the women) should not disobey you (the Prophet) in all just matters."

She said, "How generous! What could be more beautiful than that, which you are inviting us to?"

And when she heard, "And they shall not kill their children," she said, "We reared them when they were young until they grew up, and then you and your companions killed them at Badr." 'Umar b. al-Khattab chuckled so hard that his body stooped.

When the prophet (pbuh) said (quoting the Qur'an), *"They (the women) should not bring forth a slander they have invented between their arms and legs."* She said, "By God, Uttering a slander is disgraceful, but it is sometimes better to ignore it."

Then the Prophet (pbuh) told 'Umar, "Take their oath", and he asked God to forgive them.

(The Prophet [pbuh] never shook hands with a woman who was not his wife or a member of his immediate family.)

[Note the following verse from the Quran]:

"O Prophet! When believing women come to you to take the oath of fealty to you, that they will not associate in worship any other thing whatever with God, that they will not steal, that they will not commit adultery (or fornication), that they will not kill their children, that they will not utter slander, intentionally forging falsehood, and that they will not disobey you in any just matter; then accept their pledge, and pray to God for the forgiveness (of their sins), for God is Oft-Forgiving, Most Merciful. O you who believe! Take not as friends the people who incurred the Wrath of Allah. Surely, they have been in despair to receive any good in the Hereafter, just as the disbelievers have been in despair about those (buried) in graves (that they will not be resurrected on the Day of Resurrection)." (60: 12-13)

THE PROPHET (PBUH) PREPARES TO FACE THE HAWAZIN TRIBE

The Prophet (pbuh) headed toward the tribe of Hawazin, and Safwan b. Umayya, then a non-Muslim, was with him. The Prophet asked Safwan to lend him his weapons, a hundred shields with their accompanying arms. Safwan asked him, "By force or by choice?" The Prophet (pbuh) said, "We want to borrow them, and guarantee to return them." So Safwan lent the weapons to the Prophet (pbuh), who asked him to carry them with him to Hunayn. Safwan witnessed the campaigns of Hunayn and Taif. Then the Messenger of God (pbuh) came back to Alji'rana. As the Prophet (pbuh) was walking by the war booty along with Safwan, the latter started looking at the valley that was full of livestock, and he could not turn away his eyes from

71

the spectacle. All the time, the Prophet (pbuh) was watching him. He said, "Abu Wahab, do you like this valley?" Safwan said, "Yes." The Prophet (pbuh) said, "It is all yours, and whatever is in it." Then Safwan said, "No one can be pleased with giving something like this except a prophet. I bear witness that there is no deity except God, and that Muhammad is His slave and messenger. "Safwan became Muslim.

PRAYER FOR TOUGH ENEMIES, BANU THAQIF

Jabir reports that some of the Prophet's (pbuh) companions said, "O Messenger of God, the arrows of Thaqif afflicted us severely. Do make a prayer for their destruction." He said, "O Lord, guide Thaqif!"

DISTRIBUTING THE SPOILS OF THE BATTLE OF HUNAYN

The Prophet Muhammad (pbuh) obtained much silver as booty (from the battle of Hunayn), four thousand ounces. All the booty was brought to the Prophet (pbuh) . Abu Sufyan b. Harb brought the silver in front of him. He said, "Messenger of God, you have become the richest among the Quraish." The Prophet (pbuh) smiled. Then Abu Sufyan said, "Give me some of this, Messenger of God?" The Prophet (pbuh) said, "Bilal, weigh forty ounces of silver for Abu Sufyan and give him a hundred camels." Abu Sufyan said, "What about my son Yazid?" The Prophet (pbuh) said, "Weigh for Yazid forty ounces of silver and give him a hundred camels." Abu Sufyan said, "And my son Muawiyah, Messenger of God." The Prophet (pbuh) said, "Weigh for him, O Bilal, forty ounces of silver and give him a hundred camels."

Abu Sufyan said, "You are indeed generous! May my parents be sacrificed for your sake. I fought you and you were the most honorable of foes, and I have made peace with you and you have proved to be the best of those who are peaceful. May God reward you with his best blessings." The Prophet (pbuh) also gave gifts to the tribe of Asad.

THE GIFTS CONTROVERSY

On the authority of Amr b. Taghlib, "The Prophet (pbuh) made large gifts to some people while denying others. Some of them felt aggrieved. So he said, 'I give out gifts to certain people because I fear that they may be shaken. Others I entrust to what God has placed in their hearts of goodness and contentment. Among the latter is Amr b. Taghlib.'" Amr b. Taghlib said, "I would not exchange the Prophet's (pbuh) statement for red camels."

TALK OF DISSENT FROM THE ANSAR

Abu Sa'id al-Khudri reports: "When the Prophet (pbuh) distributed the booty as gifts to Quraish and the other Arab tribes, he gave nothing to the Ansar. A portion of the Ansar developed a grudge and began spreading rumors. One of them finally said, 'The Messenger of God has returned to his people.'

Sa'ad b Ubadah (the chief of the Ansar), went to the Prophet (pbuh) and said, 'Messenger of God, some of the Ansar have taken your action to heart; the way you have distributed the spoils of war amongst your people and the other Arabian tribes. No such gifts were made to any persons of the Ansar.'

The Prophet (pbuh) asked, 'What is your own stand, O Sa'ad?'

Sa'ad replied, 'I am only one of my people. And who am I?'

The Prophet (pbuh) said 'Assemble your people over there. Sa'ad left and gathered the people at that place. Some men among the Muhajiroon (the immigrants) also came, and he let them enter. Others came, and he turned them away. When all of them were gathered, Sa'ad came (to the Prophet [pbuh]) and said, 'A group of the Ansar is assembled for you.'

The Prophet (pbuh) went out to them. He praised God and glorified Him as He should be glorified. He then said, 'O people of Ansar, A rumor concerning you has reached me, and so has your grievance. Did I not come to you when you were astray, and God has directed you to the right path?

And were you not poor, and God gave you wealth? Did I not come to you when you were enemy one to another, and God has united your hearts?' They answered, 'Indeed, God and His Messenger have been most generous, and are better than all else.'

He said, 'Why do you not respond to me, people of Ansar?'

They replied, 'How should we answer you, O Messenger of God? We are greatly indebted to God and his Messenger.'

The Prophet (pbuh) said, 'By God, if you wish you can say what is true and what people will believe.'

They said, 'You came to us when others had rejected and belied you and we accepted you. You were forsaken and we supported you; you were a fugitive, and we took you in; you were indigent, and we took care of you.'

'People of the Ansar,' rsponded the Prophet (pbuh), 'you are aggrieved at the trifle of this world which I have given out to certain people in order to reconcile some people's hearts, so that they incline toward peace, while I left you to the strength of your faith. Are you not pleased, O people of the Ansar, that other people should go back to their homes with sheep and camels while you go back to yours in the company of God's Messenger? By Him who holds Muhammad's soul in His hands, had it not been for my emigration I would have been one of the Ansar. If the people took a path through the valley, and the Ansar took another, truly will I take the path of the Ansar. O God, shower your mercy on the Ansar, and the children of the Ansar and the children of their children.'

The people wept until their beards were drenched in tears. They said, 'We are satisfied with God's Messenger as our share, as our fortune.' The Prophet (pbuh) left and we dispersed."

SPECULATING ON THE PROPHET'S (PBUH) NEW RESIDENCE

Imam Muslim narrates on the authority of Abu Huraira the hadith relating to the fath (opening) of Makkah, in which it is related that the Ansar said to each other, "The man probably has a new desire to return to his place of birth and his people."

We answered, 'Yes, we did say so.' He said, 'By no means! I am only a Servant of God and His Messenger. I migrated to God and to you. My living will be with you, and so will be my dying.' We came toward him weeping and saying, 'By God, we only said what we said because we are jealous on God's account and on yours.' He said, 'Truly, God and His Messenger believe you, and forgive you.'

ANOTHER VERSION (Riwaya Ibn Hisham)

Ibn Hisham relates that on the day the Prophet (pbuh) opened and entered Makkah, he stood on Safa (a small hill by the Ka'aba) and started supplicating to God. The Ansar, who were watching him, said, "Now that God has given the Messenger his own land and his own city, do you think that he will settle here?" When he had finished his prayer, he asked, "What did you say?" They said, "Nothing, O Messenger of God." He kept on asking the same question until they told the truth. The Prophet (pbuh) then said, "I seek the refuge of God, my life is life with you, and I shall die while I am with you."

~

Chapter Three

From the Opening of Makkah to his Death

A CHRISTIAN DELEGATION FROM
NAJRAN VISITS THE PROPHET (EXCERPTS)

The Christian delegation from Najran headed toward Madinah to meet with the Prophet. When they reached Madinah, they took off their traveling clothes and put on flowing garments of rich fabric and rings of gold. Then they continued their journey until they came to the Messenger of God. They greeted him, but he did not respond. They kept addressing him all day, but he would not respond. They still had on their magnificent robes and rings of gold. Then they went looking for 'Uthman b. Affan and 'Abd al-Rahman b. 'Auf, who used to travel in caravans to Najran for trade before Islam. They used to buy wheat, dates and corn in Najran. The Najran delegates found them among the Ansar and the Muhajiroon. They said, "O 'Uthman, O 'Abd al-Rahman, your Prophet (pbuh) sent us a letter, and here we are in response. We have greeted him, but he would not respond. We kept on eliciting his speech all day long until we despaired. What then should we do, in your opinion? Should we return to Najran?" 'Abdul Rahman and 'Uthman asked Ali, "What should we tell these people, O Father of Hassan?" Ali said, "I think that they should take off their ornate garments and rings, and dawn on their travel clothes." The delegation did as advised, returned to the Messenger of God, and greeted him, and he returned their greetings. Then he added, "By the One Who sent me, when they came to me the first time, Iblis (Satan) was in their company."

Then he asked them questions, and they also asked him questions on religious doctrine. They continued thus until they asked him, "What do you say about Jesus? We will return to our people, and as we are Christians, if indeed you are a Prophet (pbuh) , we will be very happy to know what you have to say about him."

The Prophet said, "I have nothing to say about him today. You have to stay until I can tell you what will be said to me about Jesus." By the time he woke up the next day, the following verses had been revealed to him:

"Jesus in God's sight is like Adam. He created him from dust and said to him 'Be' and he was. The truth is from your Lord. Do not, therefore, be among those in doubt. If anyone argues with you about him after what has been given to you of true knowledge, say to them, 'Let us invite our children and your children, our women and your women, and ourselves and yourselves. Let us then all pray to God, and ask that God's curse overwhelm those who are not speaking the truth.'" (3: 59-61)

They refused to sign on to this.

When the Messenger of God woke up the following morning, he came to the assembly flanked by his grandsons, Hassan and Hussein. His daughter Fatima walked behind him. They came for the oath (mentioned above). He also had a number of wives at that time.

Then Shurahbil said to his two companions, "'Abdullah b. Shurahbil and Jabbar b. Fayd, the two of you know that our valley—the lower portion of it, and the upper—will only act based on my opinion. I feel that the matter is grave indeed. If this man is a king, and we are the first of the Arabs to reject his authority and challenge him, he will always harbor a grudge against us. He and his people will not stop until they inflict defeat upon us. We live in proximity to his domain more than any other Arab group. And if he is truly a Prophet and a Messenger of God, and we exchange curses with him, doom will befall us to the last hair and the last nail."

The two men rejoined, "What do you say then? You do not have an easy way out there." Shurahbil said, "My opinion is that we accept his judgment. I see him as a man who would never judge unfairly." They said, "We accept your ruling." So Shurahbil met with the Messenger of God and said, "I have a better way than exchanging curses with you." "What is it?" the Messenger of God asked.

Shurahbil answered, "Take the whole day till the evening, and the whole night till the morning, to come up with a verdict in our case. We shall accept whatever you decide."

The Prophet (pbuh) said to him, "There may be someone back home who would blame you for this." Shurahbil said, "Ask my two companions." He asked them and they said, "The people of the valley will take no decision except based on the opinion of Shurahbil." The Prophet (pbuh) then remarked, "One who rejects the faith enters into an agreement (with me)." The Messenger of God called off the oath taking.

The following morning, he came and had someone write an agreement with Najran. The Prophet (pbuh) stipulated the jizya (the poll tax), which the people of Najran would be paying to the Muslim Government. "In return, Najran and its people come under the sacred protection of God and Muhammad, the Prophet (pbuh). He (Muhammad) pledges to protect their lives, their religion, and no bishop will lose his title, and no monk will lose his monastic traditions, and no dweller in a house bearing a cross lose his rank and practices."

THE AZDI DELEGATION

Alqama b. Yazid b. Suwayd al-Azdi said: "My father narrated to me what he heard from my grandfather Suwayd b. al-Harith, who said, 'I was one of seven people from our tribe, who traveled as a delegation to meet with the Messenger of God. When we came into his presence and spoke to him, he was pleased with our manners and style of clothes. He asked, 'What are you?' We said, 'Believers.' The Prophet (pbuh) smiled and said, 'Every statement must have substance. What is the substance of your statement and your beliefs?' We said, 'Fifteen characteristics. Five of which your messengers asked us to believe in; five we were to practice (as Muslims); and five were part of our moral code, prior to Islam, which we still maintain, except if you object to any of them.'

The Prophet (pbuh) asked, 'What are the five in which my messengers have asked you to believe?' We said, 'They taught us to believe in God, His angels, His books, His messengers and in resurrection after death.' The Prophet asked, 'What are the five that they have asked you to practice?' We said, 'They have taught us to declare that there is no deity other than God, to attend regularly to our prayers, to pay Zakat, fast in the month of Ramadan and offer pilgrimage to the House if we are able to do so.'

The Prophet (pbuh) then asked us, 'And what are the five which you had before Islam?' We said, 'Gratitude in times of ease; patience in times of trial; acceptance of the turns of fate; commitment and dedication when we meet the enemy; and not rejoicing at the misfortunes of our enemy.' The Prophet (pbuh) exclaimed, 'Scholars! Sages! By their good judgment, they are almost prophets!'

He then said, 'I am adding five more qualities so that you have twenty in all. If you are truly as you have described, then do not accumulate what you cannot eat. Do not build houses you do not live in. Do not compete over something you are leaving behind tomorrow. Have fear of God to whom you shall return and be accountable to. Desire what you are moving toward, and the state in which you shall remain forever.' The people left the company of the Messenger of God. We learned his advice very well, and lived by it.'"

THE BAHRAA TRIBE DELEGATION

Karima Bint al-Miqdad said: "I heard my mother, Duba'a Bint al-Zubair b. Abd al-Muttalib, saying, 'The Bahara delegation came to the Messenger of God from Yemen. They were thirteen men. They came pulling their mounts until they arrived at the home of al-Miqdad. We were at home, in the house of Hudaila. al-Miqdad came out to meet them and welcomed them to his home. He brought them a bowl of grounded dates. We had been preparing it so that we could sit and eat. That was before they arrived. al-Miqdad, who was very generous with food, took it (to them). They ate of it until they were satisfied and the bowl was returned to us. It had some food that we poured into a smaller bowl, and we sent Sidra, my slave-girl, with it to the Messenger of God. She found him in the house of Umm Salama (his wife). The Messenger of God said, 'Did Duba'a send this?' Sidra answered, 'Yes, O Messenger of God.' He said, 'Put it down.' He added, 'What happened to the guests of Abu Ma'abad (al-Miqdad)?' I replied, 'They are at our place.'

The Messenger ate some of it along with those with him in the house, who ate until they were satisfied. Sidra ate with them. Then the Prophet (pbuh) said, 'Take what remains back to your guests.' Sidra said, 'I returned with what remained in the bowl to my master. The guests kept eating of the same food as long as they stayed with us, and it never decreased in quantity.' People started saying, 'O Abu Ma'abad, you are serving us the most beloved food to us, which we can afford to eat only rarely. We had been informed that the usual good food in your country is a rarity, or nearly so, and here we are well fed in your house!'

Abu Ma'abad informed them about what the Messenger of God did (with the food); that is that he had eaten some of it and returned what remained. This shows the blessedness of the fingers of the Messenger of

God (with which he ate). The people then said, 'We bear witness that he is he Messenger of God.' Their faith became certainty. And that is what the Messenger of God had wanted.

They then learned the obligations of the faith. They stayed with us four days, and then went to the Messenger of God to bid him farewell. He asked that they be given gifts, and they headed back home to their people.'"

THE FAREWELL PILGRIMAGE: FAREWELL SERMON (EXCERPTS)

Abu Hurra al-Raqashi narrates on the authority of his uncle who said: "I was holding the reins of the Messenger of God's she-camel during the days of tashriq (during pilgrimage). I was protecting him (the Messenger of God) from the crowd. He said, 'O People, do you know what month this is; and what day this is; and what place this is?' They replied, 'A Sacred month, and a sacred day and a sacred place.'

He went on, 'Know that your blood, your wealth and your honor are sacred among you, just as this month, this day and this place are sacred to you.' He then said, 'Listen carefully and you will thrive. Do not oppress! Do not oppress! Do not oppress! A man's wealth is his (can not be taken by another), except what he freely parts with. Surely all the blood vendettas, illegal taking of wealth, and all dealings in usury practiced during the days of ignorance (before Islam) are now under those feet of mine (abrogated) until the Day of Judgment.

The first blood vendetta I nullify is that of b. Rabi'a b. al-Harith b. Abd al-Muttalib, who was nursed in the Laith tribe, and was killed by Hudhail.

All usury of the days of ignorance is abrogated and prohibited. God has decreed that the first interest claims to be nullified are those of Abbass b. Abd al-Muttalib. You are entitled to your original capital. Do not oppress, and do not be oppressed!

After I am gone, do not revert to disbelief striking each other's necks (in war). Truly Satan has lost all hopes that people who pray to God (Muslims) will ever worship him, but he will try to sow dissension among you.

Fear God with regards to your wives. For they are as it were powerless captives. They have certain rights over you; and you have certain rights over them.

Whoever has been entrusted with something should fulfill that trust. He then stretched out his hands and said, 'Have I conveyed (the message)? Have I conveyed the message?' Then he said, 'Let those present, convey to those not here (what I have said). For it happens that the one to whom a message is relayed comprehends it better than the one who first heard it.'"

ADDRESSING THE COMMUNITY AFTER
VISITING THE MARTYRS OF UHUD

Uqbah b. 'Amir relates that the Messenger of God went out one day and offered his usual prayers for the dead for his companions who died at the Uhud battle. Then he climbed the pulpit and said, "I will go ahead of you, and I am a witness upon you. And by God, I can see my fountain in Paradise right now. And I have been offered the keys of the treasuries of the earth, or the keys of the earth. By God I certainly do not fear that you will associate partners with God (again) after I am gone. But I fear that you will compete in them (amassing of worldly wealth)."

THE CONGREGATION WAITS FOR
THE PROPHET TO LEAD THEM IN PRAYER

Ubaidullah b. 'Abdullah b. Utba said: "I entered the home of 'A'isha and said (to 'A'isha), 'Please, tell me about the condition of the Messenger of God.' She said, 'The Prophet has become heavy (i.e. seriously ill).' The Prophet (pbuh) asked, 'Have the people prayed?' We said, 'No, they are waiting for you.' He said, 'Pour water for me in a pan.' She ('Aisha) said, 'We have done so.' He took a bath and tried to get up, but fell unconscious. When he regained consciousness he asked, 'Have the people prayed?' We said, 'No Prophet of God, they are waiting for you.' He said, 'Pour water for me in the pan.' He sat down and took a bath, and tried to get up, but fell unconscious. Then he regained consciousness and asked, 'Have the people prayed?' We said, 'No Prophet of God, they are waiting for you.'

He said, 'Pour water for me in the pan.' He sat down and took a bath, and tried to get up, but fell unconscious. Then he regained consciousness and asked, 'Have the people prayed?' We said, 'No Prophet of God, they are waiting for you.'

(All the while) the people were in their prayer posture in the mosque waiting for the Prophet (pbuh), to come and lead them in the Isha (Night prayer). Then the Prophet (pbuh) sent for Abu Bakr, and asked him to lead the people in prayer. The envoy reached him and said, 'The Messenger of God has asked you to lead the people in prayer.' Abu Bakr, who was an emotional man, said, 'O 'Umar, lead the people in prayer.' 'Umar said to him, 'You are more qualified to do so.' So, Abu Bakr led the prayer during those days (of the Prophet's [pbuh] illness). On one occasion, the Prophet (pbuh) felt somewhat better, so he left his room supported by two men, one of whom was Abbass, and headed for the prayer hall for the noon prayer. Abu Bakr was leading the prayer. Upon seeing him, Abu Bakr moved backward to cede the leadership place to the Prophet (pbuh). The Prophet (pbuh) signaled to him not to move back. He said (to those supporting him), 'Place me beside him.' So they made him sit by Abu Bakr. Abu Bakr started praying with the intention of being led by the Prophet (pbuh) in the prayer, while the people went on praying believing that Abu Bakr was leading the prayer. And the Prophet (pbuh) prayed seated."

THE PROPHET MAKES A DEATHBED REQUEST

Ibn Abbass relates from al-Fadl b. Abbass saying:

"The Prophet came to my dwelling, and I came out (to meet him). He was sick, and there was a band round his head. He said, 'Take me by the hand, Fadl.' I took his hand and led him to the pulpit, where he sat and said, 'Call the people!' I called the people, and they gathered around him. He thanked his Lord and praised Him. He offered himself and invited the people to repay any injuries he might have inflicted on them, and went on to say:

If I have ever beaten any of you on his back, let him come and avenge himself by beating me on the back. If I ever insulted anyone, and attacked his honor let him come and insult me, and attack my honor. No one should say that I fear that the Messenger of God has rancor towards me. Indeed, Quarrel and enmity are not part of my nature, nor do they appeal to me. Truly, the one dearest to me is the one whom I owe something and claims it from me, or releases me from that obligation; has a right against me and claims it. By so doing, he allows me to meet God in good spirits with nothing held against me by any person. I do not think saying that will be sufficient for me until I stand up to address you several times ' Then he came down and prayed Zuhr (Noon prayer)."

THE PROPHET WATCHES THE MUSLIMS PRAYING THROUGH THE CURTAIN OF HIS ROOM

Ibn Shihab said on the authority of Anas: "It was Yaum al-Ithnain (Monday), and the Muslims were doing their morning prayer led by Abu Bakr. Nothing distracted them from their prayers; were it not that the Prophet had lifted the curtain of 'A'isha's room (where he was). He watched them as they were lined up in prayer. He smiled and then laughed (softly).

Abu Bakr stepped back to join the line, thinking that the Messenger of God wanted to join the prayer. Anas said, 'The Muslim's prayerful concentration was put to a test as a result of their joy at seeing the Prophet. So the Prophet signaled to them with his hand as if to say: 'Go on and complete your prayer.' Then he entered the room again and drew down the curtain."

An Unforgettable Detail for 'A'isha

'A'isha used to say: "Out of God's Grace, the Messenger of God died in my house, during the day of my turn while he was leaning against my chest, and that God made it possible for my saliva and his saliva to come together on the day he passed away.

Abd al-Rahman b. Abu Bakr had entered the room with a green miswak (used for brushing teeth) in his hand! The Prophet was leaning his weight on me. I saw him looking at it (the miswak), and I knew that he loved miswaks. I said, 'Should I get it for you?' He said, 'yes' by nodding his head. I took it, but it was hard for him. I said, 'Can I soften it for you?' He said "yes" by nodding his head. So I softened it (in my mouth). He brushed his teeth. Close to him was a container with water. He dipped his hands in the water and rubbed his face, saying, 'There is no god but God. Truly the pangs of death are intoxicating!' He then stretched forth his hand and said, "With the Highest Companion!" He kept saying this until he breathed his last, and his hand dropped slowly."

~

Chapter Four

Eyewitness Recollections on the Prophet's Character [Excerpts]

The following are excerpted from descriptions of the Prophet (both physical looks and character) made by Hind Ibn Abu Hala, Khadijah's son from an earlier marriage. His descriptions were made to Hassan, the brother of Husain, both of them being sons of the Prophet's daughter, Fatima. The description can be considered a summary of the teachings in this book.

Al-Hassan b. Ali said: "I asked my uncle, Hind b. Abu Hala (Khadijah's son from a previous marriage) to describe to me the Prophet's speaking habits. He said, 'The Messenger of God was mostly of a somber mood and the Prophet would remain engrossed in meditations continually for long spells. He seemed not to find time for rest. He never spoke needlessly, and would remain in long silence. His speech was concise. He was soft-spoken, never harsh, nor demeaning. He never saw any favor done to him as small. He would say nothing negative about a gift; and if he ate food given to him that he did not like, he would neither praise it nor criticize it.

Setbacks in worldly matters did not make him angry.

For the wrong done to him personally, he would never become angry, nor seek retribution.

When he pointed out something, he did so with his whole hand, and when he was astonished he turned his hand over. In speaking with another man, he would strike the palm of the right hand with the inside part of his left thumb. Angry, he would avert his face; joyful, he would look downwards. His laughter was but a smile.'

I concealed what I heard from al-Husain b. Ali (his brother) for a long time. When I (finally) told him about it, I discovered that he was the first to ask him (their uncle) what I asked him. In fact he had asked his father (Ali) about the Prophet's habits of entering, leaving, sitting, and about his structure. And he (Ali) had left nothing unsaid.

He said, 'I asked him (Ali) about how the Prophet conducted himself when he left his home. He said, 'The Messenger of God used to imprison his tongue, and would only speak on issues that concerned him. He used speech to reconcile people, never to divide them. He honored each tribe's notables and made them rulers over their tribes. He was cautious in his dealings with people; lest they sought to harm him. He loved to visit his friends. He asked about the mores of people, and would praise the good ones and reinforce them; and disapprove of the ugly ones. He was always moderate, and shunned extremism.

He said, "I asked him about his conduct in gatherings, and he said: 'The Messenger of God never joined or left a gathering without uttering words of remembrance (of God). When he joined a gathering, he sat wherever the circle had ended at the time of his joining it (that is so, he did not move to the front of the gathering), and taught everybody to do likewise. He honored all those who sat with him, and none of them would feel that someone else was dearer to the Messenger of God than him.

If anybody asked for something or needed his help, he never allowed him to leave without disposing of his business or at least comforted him with words, kind and sweet. Such was his grace and kindness to one and all that everybody took him as his father. All those who sat with him were given their rights and felt equal to everybody else. His gatherings were full moments of forbearance, modesty, patience and trust. Voices were not raised, and foul speech was avoided.

The aged were treated with special reverence, and the young enjoyed compassion.

He was always cheerful, easygoing, neither coarse, nor harsh. He was neither boisterous nor fault finding.

No one asking him a favor is disappointed. He avoided three things: arguing, love of wealth, delving in what does not concern him.

The three things he spared others were that he never spoke ill of anyone, nor maligned anybody, nor pried into any one's failings. He only spoke when he felt that he would get reward for it. When he spoke, all those present listened to him attentively, lowering their heads as if birds were sitting on their heads. When he stopped speaking, others would speak; and in his assemblies people did not vie for speaking. While someone spoke, everybody else listened until he was done.

He laughed on the remarks that made others laugh, and expressed surprise over things that astonished others. He put up patiently with the rude speech of strangers and their requests until his companions diverted the attention of such persons. He used to say, 'Help those whom you find in need.' He only allowed praise that was moderate. He never interrupted nor cut in the talk of others. If anybody exceeded the limits, he either forbade him or rose and left.'

He said, "I asked him about his silence, upon which he said: 'He refrained from speaking on four grounds: out of forbearance, circumspection, in order to form a correct judgment, and in order to think. As for forming a correct judgment, this is for the purpose of forming the fairest opinion about people. His thoughts and reflections focused on contemplating the transient and the eternal. He had two great attributes: forbearance and patience. Nothing made him angry or enraged him. He was particular about four matters: doing the beautiful so that others can emulate him; shunning ugly conduct so that others could avoid it; constantly thinking of ways to bring good to his community, and undertaking what it takes to bring happiness to his people in this world and in the Hereafter.

~

Chapter Five

A Short Sampling of
the Stories of the Prophet

Like many of the world's great teachers, such as Jesus the son of Mary, the Prophet Muhammad used stories to convey important teachings. Many of the stories he told to his companions are related to Biblical Prophets or to other individuals of pre-Islamic, pre-Judeo-Christian culture, whose lives inspired people to seek piety and moral excellence. The stories that he told about the prophets before him are especially important because they give more information about those figures beyond the few things the Qur'an says about them.

The Prophet Muhammad did not create the stories. He learned them from divine inspiration and simply shared them with his people for their edification.

That he chose stories related to the Jewish and Christian traditions underscores that the essential ethical conceptions of those traditions resonated with him and are in harmony with the Islamic faith.

I WILL DEFINITELY GIVE SOME CHARITY TODAY

Abu Huraira narrates that the Prophet said:

"A man said, 'I will definitely give some charity.' He went out with his charity and gave it to a thief (unwittingly).

The next morning people were saying, 'Charity has been given to a thief!' The man said (to himself), 'O Lord, to you belong all praises and thanks. I will certainly give some charity.' He went out with his charity and gave it to a fornicating woman (prostitute).

The next morning people were saying, 'Charity has been given to a prostitute!' The man said, 'O Lord, to you belong all praise and thanks. I gave charity to a prostitute. I will certainly give some charity.' He went out with his charity and gave it to a rich man.

The next morning people were saying, 'Charity has been given to a rich man!' The man said to himself, 'O Lord, to you belong all praise and thanks, on account of the thief, the prostitute, and the wealthy person!'

He then had a vision, in which he was told, 'As for your charity to a thief, it might get him out of the need to steal. As for the prostitute, it might get her to stop prostitution. As for the rich man, he might learn from this, and start giving in charity some of what God has given him.'"

"WATER THE GARDEN OF SO-AND-SO!"

Abu Huraira reported that the Prophet, may God bless him and grant him peace, said: "A man was walking in the open desert when he heard a voice in the clouds say, 'Cause water to pour down on the garden of so-and-so.'

And that cloud came down and poured out its water into a rocky area. There was a small canal that collected the water. He followed the flowing water and found a man standing in his garden directing the water with his spade. He said to him, 'Servant of God, what is your name?' He said, 'So-and-so', the same name he had heard mentioned in the cloud. The man then said to him, 'O servant of God, why did you ask me my name?' He said, 'I heard a voice in the cloud from which this water came, say, "pour water on the garden of so-and-so", giving your name. What are you doing with it?' He said, 'Since you have said this, well, I wait and see what produce comes out and give a third of it away as *sadaqa* (charity), my family and I eat one third of it, and I reinvest a third back into it.'"

CREMATE MY BODY, AND DISPERSE THE ASHES

Abu Sa'id narrates that the Prophet said that there was a man before your time whom God had blessed with wealth.

At the time of his death, he asked his sons, "What kind of father was I to you?" They said, "The best of fathers." He said, "I have not done any good (in my life). So when I die, cremate me and crush my body and scatter my ashes on a windy day." And they did. Then (God) Almighty gathered him back together—and said, "What made you do this?" He replied, "Out of fear of you." Upon this, God showered His Mercy upon him.

THE LEPER, THE BLIND MAN AND THE BALD-HEADED MAN

Abu Huraira heard the Prophet say: "God wanted to test three persons from the nation of Israel, a leper, a blind man, and a bald-headed man. So, he sent them an angel who came to the leper and said, 'What thing do you like most?' He replied, 'A more beautiful complexion and a more beautiful skin for the people have shunned me a great deal.' The angel rubbed him, his ailment disappeared, and he now had a beautiful complexion and a more beautiful skin. The angel asked him, 'What kind of wealth do you like best?' He replied, 'Camels (or cows)' (the narrator is in doubt, for either the leper or the bald-headed man demanded camels and the other demanded cows). So he (i.e. the leper) was given a pregnant she-camel, and the angel said (to him), 'May God bless you in it.'

Then the angel went to the bald-headed man and said, "What thing do you like most?' He replied, 'Beautiful hair and to be cured of this for the people have shunned me a great deal.' The angel rubbed him, his ailment disappeared, and he now had beautiful hair. The angel asked him, 'What kind of wealth do you like best?' He replied, 'Cows.' The angel gave him a pregnant cow and said, 'May God bless you in it.'

92

Then the angel went to the blind man and asked, 'What thing do you like best?' He said, '(I want) my eyesight to be restored to me to me so that I may see the people.' The angel rubbed him and God restored his eyesight. The angel asked him, "What kind of wealth do you like best?' He replied, 'Sheep.' The angel gave him a pregnant sheep.

Afterwards, the three animals delivered young ones. Each flock grew in number until one man had a valley full of camels, the other had had a valley full of cows, and the other had a valley full of sheep.

Then the angel came to the erstwhile leper in his (leper's) former appearance and said, 'I am a poor man. I have lost all the means of any sustenance during my travel. So no one can provide for my needs today except God, and then you. In the name of the One who granted you a beautiful complexion, nice skin, and wealth in camels, I ask you to give me a camel that will support me in my journey.' He replied, 'I have many responsibilities.' The angel said, 'It seems as if I know you. Were you not a leper, and people used to shun you? Weren't you poor and God granted you wealth?' He replied, 'I inherited (this wealth) from my fore-fathers, who had inherited it from their fore-fathers.' The angel said, 'If you are lying may God bring you back to your former state!'

He then came to the erstwhile bald-headed man in his former appearance, who had the same response for him as the former leper. He said to him, 'If you are lying may God bring you back to your former state!'

He then came to the erstwhile blind man in his former appearance and said, 'I am a poor man. I have lost all the means of my sustenance during my travel. So no one can provide for my needs today except God, and then you. In the name of the One who restored your eyesight I ask you to give me sheep which will be a source of sustenance for me in my journey.' He replied, 'I was once blind and God restored my eyesight, poor, and God gave me wealth.

Take, therefore (from my sheep) what you need. By God I will not make you struggle to return anything you take as I gave it for God's sake.' The angel said, 'Hold on to your wealth; you have simply been tried. And God is well pleased with you and is angry with your two companions.'"

HE HAD MURDERED NINETY-NINE PEOPLE

Abu Sa'id al-khudri narrates that the Messenger of God said:

"Among the nation of Israel there was a man who had murdered ninety-nine persons. Then he set out on a journey in order to ask scholars about his situation.

He came to a monk and asked him, 'Is forgiveness possible for me through repentance?' He replied, 'No.' So he killed him. He kept on asking people until one man told him, 'Head for village so and so.' Death met him on his way. While dying, he turned his chest towards that village (where he had hoped his repentance would be accepted). The angels of mercy and the angels of punishment disputed as to who had jurisdiction over the dead person. God then inspired the village the man had been heading toward to come closer (to the death spot) and inspired the village he was coming from, to move farther away. He then ordered them the angels to measure the two distances. They found the village of repentance to be closer by one span, and the man was forgiven."

THREE PEOPLE WENT ON A JOURNEY

Ibn 'Umar narrates that he heard the messenger of God saying:

"Three people, who lived before you, left on a journey. They sought shelter in a cave and entered it. A rock on the mountain above got loose and glided to the mouth of the cave and blocked it. They said, 'You will not be saved from (the danger posed by) this rock except by supplicating to God on the basis of your righteous deeds in the past.'

94

So one of them said, 'O Lord, I once had two old parents. I used to offer them milk before any of my family or slaves. One day by chance I was delayed and I came late. By the time I returned, they had slept. I had gotten them milk as their evening drink, but they were already sleeping.

As I hated to put wealth or family ahead of them, I waited until the start of dawn for them to wake up. All the while, I had the goblet in my hand. When they awoke, they drank their milk. O Lord, if I did this seeking your pleasure, save us from the trouble we now face with this stone. The stone then moved, but not enough for them to get out of the cave.'

The other man said, 'O Lord, I once had a female cousin. She was the most beloved person to me in the world. I desired her, but she would not let me. One year, she had a hard time in a famine year, and needed help. She came to me and I gave her one hundred-twenty dinars (money) on the condition that she puts herself at my disposal. She complied. And when I was in the position to get from her what I wanted, she said, 'I do not permit you to break the shield without you first fulfilling its obligations (through marriage).' I stopped myself at that point from having intercourse with her. And she was the most beloved person to me. I let her have the gold I had given to her. O Lord, if I did this seeking your pleasure, save us from the trouble we now face with this stone. The stone then moved, but not enough for them to get out (of the cave).'

The third person said, 'I once hired workers, and I gave to each of them his wages, except for one, who left without taking his wage. I invested his wage until it multiplied. He came back after a while and said, 'O servant of God, give me my wage.' I said, 'All that you see (right now); camels, cows, sheep and slaves are your wage.' He said, 'O servant of God, don't jest with me.' I said, 'I am not jesting with you.' So he took everything and went out with it; he left nothing behind. O Lord, if I did this seeking your pleasure, save us from the trouble we now face with this stone. The stone then moved, and they moved out walking."

~

Chapter Six

A Short Sampling of
the Prophet's Supplications

INTRODUCTION

*A*d'iya (supplications) were a very important dimension of the Prophet's life.

The moment he received the prophetic call, his entire life became perpetually immersed in spiritual awareness and remembrance of God. He would be in deep contemplation of the divine, even as he was doing something as mundane as wearing his sandals or stepping out of his house. He attained the station of *Zikr* (remembrance), a state of being for which the Qur'an reserves the highest commendation.

The Ad'iya are a type of *Zikr*, done mostly to ask God for His bounties. While the five daily prayers are the most visible form of prayer among Muslims, the most wide-spread are the supplications, which are mostly private and nurture the Muslim's personal connection to God. Through them the Muslim speaks to God in any language, as a Master with a mighty treasury of gifts, which the servant is badly in need of, or as a Friend who is ever pleased to see the jewel of His creation come to seek the solace of His Fellowship.

The Prophet Muhammad addressed His Lord through Arabic, his native language. The words he used, the powerful effect those words had on him and others, have led Muslims over the centuries to adopt them to their own individual situations. Using those words is also a way of forming a personal connection with the Prophet, and joining a community of supplicants that transcends time and space.

The stories and teachings you have read in this book have introduced you to a universe of understanding and values. The supplications of the Prophet Muhammad will hopefully take you to the heart of that universe: a man, alone in private conversation with His Creator.

GRANT ME THE GIFT OF YOUR LOVE

'Abdullah b. Yazid al-Khatmi al-Ansari narrates that the Messenger of God used to say in his supplications: "O Lord, Grant me the gift of your Love, and the love of those whose love will benefit me in your consideration. O Lord, whatever you have blessed me to love, make it strength for me in that which You love. O Lord, what you have taken away from me of what I desire, fill the empty space it left in my heart with desire for what you Love."

PRAYER FOR THE SICK

'A'isha narrates that when the Messenger of God visited a sick person, or when one was brought to him, he would say: "O Lord of Mankind! Take away this pain and grant health, for You are the giver of health. There is no health but the health that You grant, the health which leaves no sickness afterwards."

Prayer for the Heart and the Mind

Zaid b. Arqam reported: I am not going to say anything but only that which God's Messenger used to say. He used to supplicate:" O Allah, I seek refuge in You from incapacity, from laziness, from cowardice, from miserliness, decrepitude and from torment of the grave. O Lord, make my soul righteous. Purify it, for You are the best to purify it. For you are its Protecting Friend and Master. Lord, I seek your protection from knowledge that does not benefit, and from a heart that does not throb, and from a soul that can not be satisfied, and from supplications that are not answered."

Prayer of Distress

'Abdullah b Jaafar said: "When Abu Talib died, the Prophet traveled to Taif on foot in order to call them (the people of Taif) to Islam. They did not heed his call (they unleashed boys on him to pelt him with stones, which left him bleeding). He therefore fled and came to the shade provided by a tree, and did two units of prayer (*rakatain*). He then supplicated:

'O God, I complain to you of the feebleness of my ability, the scarcity of my means, and my humiliation before the people.

You are the source of all mercy, the Lord of the weak, and my Master.

With whom shall you entrust my care? Shall you entrust it with a stranger who will treat me with contempt, or have you granted an enemy, power to dispose of my affairs?

If You are not angry with me, nothing else matters. But I stand in greater need of your compassionate Grace.

I seek protection in the light of Your countenance, on whose account all darkness gives way to light, and all affairs of the world and the Hereafter are rectified.

This is better for me than that your anger descends upon me, or that your displeasure should overwhelm me.

I will linger at your doorstep until you show your pleasure.

There is no power, and no strength except in you (and through you).'"

PROTECT ME FROM LETHARGY, COWARDICE, SENILITY AND STINGINESS

Anas b Malik narrates that the Messenger of God used to seek protection thus:

"O Lord, I seek your protection from lethargy;

I seek your protection from cowardice;

I seek your protection from the decrepitude of old age;

I seek your protection from stinginess."

WE HAVE HEARD THE CALL

"Our Lord! We have heard the call of one calling (us) to Faith—"Believe you in the Lord—and we have believed. Our Lord! Forgive us our sins and expiate from us our evil deeds, and take our souls in the company of the righteous." (3: 193)

SUPPLICATIONS AFTER A PRESCRIBED PRAYER

Anas b. Malik relates: "My position during prayers is between the two shoulders of the Messenger of God. After saying *'Assalamu alaikum'* at the end a prayer, he would supplicate, saying, 'O Lord, make the best part of my life its last portion. Lord, make the crown of my good deeds your Pleasure. Lord, make the best of my days the day I shall meet with You!'"

SUPPLICATIONS AT THE END OF A GATHERING

Khalid b. Abu 'Imran reports that Ibn 'Umar relates: "The Messenger of God would not get up at the end of a gathering before saying, 'Our Lord grant us a gift of the fear of you which will stand between us and our desire to disobey You; and a gift of obedience to you that will take us to your Paradise; and certainty of faith which will make all worldly calamities easy to bear.

O Lord, secure our hearing, our eyesight and our strength for as long as we are alive. Let them survive us. Support our struggle against those who oppress us, and help us against our enemies. And do not grant power over us to those who will have no mercy on us.'"

RECTIFY MY SITUATION HERE AND IN THE HEREAFTER

Abu Huraira narrates that the Messenger of God used to pray thus: "O God rectify my religion, which is a security of my affairs, and rectify my situation in the world, in which lies my sustenance; and rectify my hereafter, which is my final abode; and make the continuation of my life an increase in all that is good for me, and death a release from all that is evil."

MAKE MY INNER-SELF BEAUTIFUL TOO!

Ibn Mas'ood narrates that the Messenger of God used to say: "O Lord, you have made my outer appearance beautiful. Please make my inner self beautiful also."

TRAVELER'S SUPPLICATION

Abu al-Zubair reports that Ali al-Azdi informed him, Ibn 'Umar taught them that whenever the Messenger of God had mounted his ride for a journey, he would say three times 'Allahu Akbar (God is the greatest)' and then, 'Glory to the One, who subjected this (mount) to our purposes. We would otherwise not have been companions (of the journey). And our return is certainly to our Lord. O Lord, we seek from You in our journey goodness, piety, and actions that please You.'

'O God! Make this journey of ours easy and shrink for us its distance. O God! You are our Companion in this journey and the Caretaker of the family (we left behind). O God! I ask for your protection from the hardship of the journey, the unpleasant sights, and the loss of family and wealth.' (upon returning recite the same again, adding): '...We return repentant to our Lord, worshipping our Lord, and praising our Lord.'

EVENING AND MORNING SUPPLICATIONS

'Abdullah b. Mas'ood narrates that the Messenger of God used to pray thus at the end of the day: "This night has come upon us in a state in which we and the entire universe are God's. All praises belong to Him.

There is no god except Him. He is one. He has no partner. To Him belongs the Dominion. He has power over all things. O God! I ask you for the good of this night and the good in it. And I seek your protection from its evil, and the evil in it. Lord, I seek your protection from lethargy, the decrepitude of old age and senility. O God! Protect me against the trial of this world, and the agony of the grave."

And in the morning he would likewise say: 'This morning comes upon us, and wakes us in a state in which we, and the entire universe, are God's.'

And Abu Bakr al-Sidiq said: "The Messenger of God asked me to say in the morning, and in the evening, and when I go to bed at night, 'O God, Creator of the heavens and the earth, Knower of the visible and the invisible, You are the Lord and Sovereign of everything. I bear witness that there is no deity except You alone, without partner; and that Muhammad is your servant and messenger. I seek refuge in you from the evil of my soul; and from the evil of Satan, and his call to associate others (with You); and from committing wrong that will harm my soul; and from causing thereby harm to a Muslim.'"

LIGHT IN MY HEART

Ibn Abbass narrates: "The Messenger of God spent a night at the house of my aunt, Maimuna. During that night he made the following supplication: 'O God, let there be light in my heart for me, and light in my tongue, and light in my ears; and light in my eyes; and light above me; and light beneath me; and light to my right; and light to my left, and in front of me light; and behind me light; and in my soul light. O Lord, make magnificent the light you grant me!'"

Surely, this is My way, leading straight. Follow it and follow not (other) paths; they will scatter you about from His (great) path. Thus does He command you, so that you may be righteous.

~

The Author

Ahmed Sheikh Bangura was born in Sierra Leone, where he did his undergraduate studies. He earned a PhD in Comparative Literature from the University of Alberta in 1994. In 2017, he took early retirement from the University of San Francisco, where he had been a professor since 1994, and had taught courses in French, Literature, Islamic studies and Arabic. His first book, *Islam and West African Fiction: The Politics of Representation* (Lynne Rienner 2000), was a work in literary criticism. More recently, he co-authored *Ayyam al-Habbib (The Days and Times of the Beloved)* of which *Indelible Footprints* is an abridged translation

He is also the founder and chair of the Ihsan Foundation for West Africa.

Made in the USA
Las Vegas, NV
30 April 2021